Appropriate Adults and Appropriate Adult Services:
Service user, provider and police perspectives

Edited by

Brian Littlechild

VENTURE PRESS

BASW website: http://www.basw.co.uk

Published by
VENTURE PRESS
16 Kent Street
Birmingham
B5 6RD

British Library Cataloguing-in-Publication Data
A catalogue record for this book is available from the British Library

ISBN: 1 86178 044 3 (paperback)

Cover design by:
Western Arts
194 Goswell Road
London
EC1V 7DT

Printed in Great Britain

Acknowledgements

I would like to thank all the volunteers and their managers for giving up their time to contribute to this book. Their dedication and commitment of the volunteers to those who need their services at a very stressful and difficult time, with little public recognition, is a healthy reminder of the enduring qualities of a spirit of community and passion for justice for people who are in difficulties.

In particular, thank you to Anne Le Fevre, manager of the NCH Action for Children Appropriate Adult Scheme, whose welcome to her area and work was so much appreciated.

The participation of the three users of services who gave of their time and experiences, who cannot be named for reasons of confidentiality, has been invaluable in trying to keep the proper focus of our work where it should - from the perspective of those who rely on our services.

Contents

Chapter 1
Introduction
Brian Littlechild

This book came about as a result of discussions amongst a wide variety of people – police, social workers, scheme managers, volunteers and academics – involved in the provision, development and evaluation of Appropriate Adult services. They all shared a concern for the experiences of the different vulnerable groups detained by police, and the benefits and problems of the use of Appropriate Adults in obtaining a just outcome from this stage of criminal proceedings for those groups defined as vulnerable and in need of Appropriate Adults to be secured by the police, as defined by the Codes of Practice produced under the 1984 Police and Criminal Evidence Act (PACE). A British Association of Social Workers' conference in 1997 (BASW 1997) explored the problems of Appropriate Adult provision and practice, and joint work on a number of these issues between the Hertfordshire Constabulary and the University of Hertfordshire identified areas in which further knowledge for, and guidance to, custody officers and Appropriate Adults was needed.

The main focus of this book is to examine these benefits and problems from a review of the research literature, and to gain a greater understanding of different perspectives on the Appropriate Adult role from all the groups involved in the delivery and use of Appropriate Adult schemes. These perspectives can then inform us of how the provision of Appropriate Adults can be improved.

The publication starts with an overview of the development of the Appropriate Adult role and some of the strengths and weaknesses of the current state of its uneven provision. It also explores the possible effects on those detained by the police. A number of the miscarriages of justice as identified in case law relevant to the provision of Appropriate Adults will also be examined in relation to people with mental health problems, learning disabilities and young people under the age of seventeen. These groups are all defined as vulnerable groups in the Codes of Practice (Home Office, 1995) for whom the police are required to secure the attendance of an Appropriate Adult. From these cases we can begin to gauge more fully what actions are appropriate in the role, and who is and who might not be an appropriate 'Appropriate Adult'.

The police are able to use relatives, or other adults not employed by the police, in the Appropriate Adult role, so there are variations across the country in relation to who acts as an Appropriate Adult, and therefore what service vulnerable detainees can expect to receive, and to what standard. This will depend upon whether they have a professional attending from one of the statutory agencies such as Social Services or Health who may or may not be trained and knowledgeable in the role, from one of the growing number of Appropriate Adult schemes, or a relative or anyone who happens to nearby at the time. The strengths and weaknesses of using Appropriate Adults from these different groups for juveniles are examined in particular in Chapters 2, 3 and 9.

The provision of Appropriate Adult schemes became particularly important in April 2000. From that time there was a requirement under the National Standards for Youth Offending Teams (Youth Justice Board, 2000) to provide Appropriate Adult schemes. The different perspectives offered in this publication will provide valuable knowledge and insights for those who set up, develop and manage such schemes.

Research and publications on the problems of the role and provision of Appropriates Adults have been produced by, amongst a small number of others, Mencap (Bean and Nemitz, 1994), the Mental Health Foundation (Palmer and Hart, 1996) the British Association of Social Workers (Littlechild, 1996), and Pearse and Gudjonsson (1996). What is new in this publication is the direct representation of the views of those involved in receiving and deliv-ering Appropriate Adult services. Two adults – one with learning disabilities and one with mental health problems – who had experienced detention and the services of Appropriate Adults gave their opinions, as did one young person of sixteen years of age.

Also new in this publication is the exploration of the experiences and views of the provision of Appropriate Adult services by those who actually deliver them: the managers and volunteers of two successful schemes in the South of England, and the experiences of custody officers whose initial role it is to try to identify those in the vulnerable groups.

With this wide variety of perspectives, this publication will be invaluable to those involved in instigating, operating and managing schemes. It will also be of value to those who act as Appropriate Adults, be this as volunteers or as staff employed in Youth Offending Teams, Probation, Health, Social Services, the voluntary sector or the Youth Service as part of their work. It will also be valuable to the police in their work, training and policies in relation to the use of Appropriate Adults (this is becoming increasingly important given the case law which has developed concerning the use of Appropriate Adults).

This then becomes important in relation to the whole of the pre-court justice system, in that it has to be demonstrated at that stage, and in subsequent proceedings, that those with vulnerabilities are treated fairly in accordance with the requirements of PACE and its Codes of Practice.

The book will be of value to those in Social Services, Youth Offending Teams and Health who are developing or buying-in their own schemes. It will also be a valuable resource in social work and health education and training courses where their areas of specialism cover mental health and/or learning disabilities, or work with young people.

Forensic Medical Examiners will also find this book of use, given their often key role in advising custody officers on vulnerability.

Overview of the chapter contents
Chapter 2 starts with an over-view of the development of the Appropriate Adult role and some of the strengths and weaknesses of the current state of varied provision and the effects on those detained by the police, including how detainees can experience the conditions of their detention, oppressive waiting times, and weak practice from those carrying out the role. A number of miscarriages of justice are examined in relation to people with mental health problems, learning disabilities and young people under the age of seventeen. There is consideration of how case law has developed concerning the use of Appropriate Adults, as prosecution cases have been dismissed in court where the judge has determined the police have not engaged the correct Appropriate Adult, have not engaged correctly with the vulnerable detainee and/or Appropriate Adult, and/or where there have been irregularities in how the Codes of Practice were implemented.

This includes situations where the Appropriate Adult fails to carry out the role correctly. This then becomes important in relation to the whole system of justice, for two reasons: first, so that those who have offended are treated fairly within the criminal justice system at all its different levels; second, where detainees who have offended are not confronted with their actions when prosecution fails because of inappropriate Appropriate Adult provision. Problematic areas in the relationships between Appropriate Adults and solicitors, and Appropriate Adults and detainees, are discussed, as are some ways of overcoming these difficulties.

In Chapter 3, John Pearse, Unit Commander in New Scotland Yard, Metropolitan Police Service, examines the development of the Appropriate Adult role from the police perspective, and the current arrangements, or lack of them, available to the police for the provision of suitable Appropriate Adults within acceptable time scales. Drawing on his own extensive research in this area during the last decade, he highlights the key problems in provision which service providers, managers, policy makers and Appropriate Adults themselves have to confront in order to provide the safeguard for vulnerable suspects which the Codes envisaged. Pearse provides examples of highly inappropriate interventions from Appropriate Adults, putting at jeopardy the detainee's rights and/or police evidence. Pearse powerfully makes the case that current provision nationwide is failing to provide the service that Parliament envisaged, and that the Government and the Home Office have failed to put in place policies or resources to ensure that consistent quality of services can be delivered. Relationships between the police and Appropriate Adult are examined. The implications of poor guidance on the role itself, including when an Appropriate Adult should attend and the need for training of police officers, are also highlighted. A screening form that may help with the identification of vulnerability is described.

In Chapter 4, Grethe Hansen explores the experiences of one man with mental health problems who has been detained by the police on a number of occasions. He gives a clear and enlightening account of his view of police and Appropriate Adult interventions. This account provides valuable insights into how those who administer schemes, the police, and those who act as Appropriate Adults can consider how they are perceived by people who are detained in order that the role can be carried out more effectively. In Chapter 5, Hansen examines how different types of mental health problem can affect the behaviour and responses of detainees, the assessment of risk, and the types of responses that may be most useful from the police and Appropriate Adult.

Chapter 6 includes the experiences of a man with learning disabilities who was detained by the police, as revealed in an interview with the chapter's author, Debra Fearns. He gives his views on how he perceived his detention, and the attitudes and interventions of the police officer and Appropriate Adult involved. What is very clear in this account is the importance of the Appropriate Adult demonstrating to the detainee and the police that the Appropriate Adult is there to ensure the welfare and well being of the detainee; however, this was not how the detainee experienced the Appropriate Adult's involvement. The chapter also examines custody officers' experiences of identifying and working with people with learning disabilities, based on Fearns' original research concerning the recognition of people with learning disabilities and subsequent provision of Appropriate Adult services. One key issue concerns how often people who are unable to read or write might be seen as learning disabled, which is of course not necessarily the case; and the importance of differentiation between those who are vulnerable due to illiteracy, and those with other needs due to their learning disability. Fearns in Chapter 7 then goes on to examine what types of behaviour and other clues might alert those providing a service to the possibility that a detainee has some type of learning disability.

Chapter 8 is based on an interview with a sixteen-year-old young person who has been detained a number of times in his home area and around the country. Again, the message comes across clearly that detainees expect Appropriate Adults to have attitudes and skills which demonstrate beyond doubt that they are there to support the detainee, and look after the detainee's welfare and interests. Each of the three interviewees had great concerns about this.

It is not claimed that the detailed exploration and exposition of three people who have been detained will give a comprehensive view of the needs of all those detained who have vulnerabilities, or that they can provide all the answers to the problems uncovered. What we are aware of, however, is that the user's perspective has been difficult to obtain from previous work, and this is a start in presenting detainees' experiences in detail, giving the opportunity to consider issues for developing practice, policy and further research.

Chapter 9 sets out how Appropriate Adult services operate (or, sometimes, fail to operate) for young people who are detained. Particular attention is given to the role of family members who act as Appropriate Adults and situations where family members have been inappropriate for the role, and why.

Chief Superintendent Keith Baldwin examines briefly in Chapter 10 the difficulties in accessing Appropriate Adults, and discusses how custody officers experience Appropriate Adults' interventions for the vulnerable groups. Police training includes little on these areas, and these types of judgement will not always be easy for those who are experienced in the filed; the police have to make these judgements with little information or chance for a full assessment. In Chapter 3, Pearse makes the point that it may be other operational considerations – for example, if the custody officer believes it may be very difficult to obtain an Appropriate Adult – which determine whether the officers will recognise a vulnerability and record it as such. This would be in accordance with Andrew Strong's experiences as set out in Chapter 11 as manager of an Appropriate Adult scheme in Southampton and the New Forest, where good access to Appropriate Adults has led to a substantial increase in requests from custody officers since the scheme has been in operation.

Chapter 11 presents the experiences and views of those who have acted as Appropriate Adults within two successful Appropriate Adult schemes in the Southampton area. One of these is operated for vulnerable adults by MIND in Southampton and the New Forest, and the other for young people, set up by NCH Action for Children. The commitment, learning and development of those involved in these schemes are instructive for developments in other parts of the country.

Andrew Strong provides the final chapter of the book, from his experience as manager for one of the first Appropriate Adult schemes for adults, instigated by Southampton and New Forest MIND. Strong sets out the advantages and the essential criteria and processes for setting up such a scheme.

Note on Codes of Practice: The Home Office Codes of Practice B–E published in 1995 remain in place. In 1999 a new code A, relating to stop and search procedures was published, but the 1999 Codes incorporate the 1995 Codes (referenced as 1995) as referred to throughout this book.

References

Bean, P and Nemitz, T (1994) *Out of Depth and Out of Sight* London, Mencap.

British Association of Social Workers (1997) A*ppropriate Adults and Vulnerable Groups in Custody: a collection of papers from a one day conference* Birmingham, BASW.

Home Office (1995) *Police and Criminal Evidence Act 1984 Codes of Practice (B-E)* London, HMSO.

Littlechild, B (1996) *The Police and Criminal Evidence Act 1984: the role of the Appropriate Adult* Birmingham, British Association of Social Workers.

Palmer, C and Hart, M (1996) *A PACE in the right direction?* Sheffield, Institute for the Study of the Legal Profession, University of Sheffield.

Pearse, J and Gudjonsson, G (1996) 'Understanding the problems of the Appropriate Adult' *Expert Evidence* 4(3), pp 101-4.

Youth Justice Board (2000) *National Standards for Youth Justice* London, Youth Justice Board.

Chapter 2
The Provision of Appropriate Adults: Practice issues
Brian Littlechild

There are a number of areas of difficulty in the provision of appropriate adults that are explored in this chapter. Problems concerning the effective implementation of the Appropriate Adult role for young people and those with mental health problems or a learning disability have been noted by a number of observers (Palmer and Hart, 1996; Pearse and Gudjonsson, 1996; Medford *et al*. 2000). There are frequently difficulties for the police in gaining the attendance of an Appropriate Adult within a reasonable time frame. Those who act as Appropriate Adults, both professionals and non-professionals, frequently fail to carry out their role effectively. The notion of vulnerability does not fit easily within the normal investigatory processes and interviewing styles of the police, which have been in part developed to overcome the resistance of non-vulnerable adults (Pearse and Gudjonsson, 1999). As one custody officer in Blackie's research stated:

> *We deal with rational people, who have chosen to do wrong and we lock them up. Suddenly we are being asked to use coercive force against people who we see as not being responsible for their actions and that does not fit easily with us.* (Blackie, 1995)

In the worst cases the detention can last for many hours before the arrival of the Appropriate Adult. Medford *et al*. (2000) found in their research that for juveniles, the average wait for an Appropriate Adult from the time they agree to attend and then actually arrive was $3\frac{1}{2}$ hours. Waits of over twelve hours after the Appropriate Adult agreed to attend were not uncommon. Where volunteers were used, the average wait was fifty-eight minutes after agreeing to attend, and the longest just over 3 hours. The longest wait was for a social worker, who took over fourteen hours to attend. Indeed, the longest waits overall were for social workers. Even more worrying, for over 5% of juveniles it was not possible for the police to gain the attendance of an Appropriate Adult at all. In 5.2 per cent (N = 186) of cases, no Appropriate Adult attended; there was evidence in 114 cases of custody officers trying to gain attendance of an appropriate adult but, in seventy two, no evidence at all of this.

For detained adults, the researchers found that 4.3 per cent of detainees were vulnerable in some way. Around 60 per cent (N = 600) were not afforded the protection and support of an Appropriate Adult. In fifty-four cases, attempts appeared to have been made to gain an appropriate adult's attendance without success; in the other 546, the vulnerability was not acknowledged and no attempt was made to gain the attendance of an Appropriate Adult, despite evidence in the custody record of the vulnerability of the detainee. The average wait for an Appropriate Adult to arrive for a vulnerable adult was nearly 6 hours, but many had waits of over twenty hours. Where volunteers or social workers were used, the average wait was just over $6\frac{1}{2}$ hours. For parents or relatives, the average wait was $5\frac{1}{2}$ hours.

These delays create significant problems for the police and the detainee. Too often the detainee will wish to escape the stress of detention as quickly as possible, and this will add to the possibility of false confessions and unreliable evidence. Detainees from amongst the vulnerable groups may not readily understand the significance of questions and how their answers to such questions will be viewed within the criminal justice system, and are likely to be more suggestible than adults who are not from those vulnerable groups.

Further considerations of the specific problems in the provision of Appropriate Adults for juveniles are explored in depth in Chapter 8. Two major problem areas for the police and detainees – recognition of vulnerability and what can lead custody officers to call an Appropriate Adult or not – are covered in further detail in the chapters by Pearse, Fearns, Hansen and Baldwin.

The purpose of the Appropriate Adult

The Appropriate Adult role was developed from a similar function required under Judges' Rules which were in place prior to the Police and Criminal Evidence Act 1984 (PACE). The role of the Appropriate Adult was first set out in the Royal Commission on Criminal Procedure in 1981 (Philips, 1981, paragraph 4.103). That stated that the Appropriate Adult's role was to 'be someone in whom the juvenile has confidence, his parents or guardian or someone else he knows, a social worker or schoolteacher'. It was considered that they might need an adult present to befriend, advise and assist them during their detention. Pearse and Gudjonsson (1996) discuss the development of the role and the lack of clarity in the Act, Codes and subsequent policies concerning how the role would work in practice.

The role of the Appropriate Adult was set out in paragraph 11.16 of the first Codes of Practice issued under PACE; they would: 'advise and assist the person being questioned and observe whether or not the interview is being conducted properly and fairly...[and] facilitate communication with the person being interviewed' (Home Office, 1985). This can be contrasted with the role of the solicitor whose duty it is to give legal advice and information. This was made explicit in the first revisions of the Codes in 1991 when it was made clear that a solicitor acting in a professional capacity could not also act as an Appropriate Adult.

The Codes of Practice have been revised twice since the original Codes, in 1991 (Home Office, 1991) and 1995 (Home Office, 1995). Helpful though they are, they were primarily written for police use and not for Appropriate Adults or suspects. Indeed, if Appropriate Adults who did not have good training and knowledge of them arrived in the police station and tried to access them to help them with their role, they would be more confusing than helpful. For a full account of the role of the Appropriate Adult, and details of the changes in the two revisions of the Codes which have had an impact on Appropriate Adult practice, see *The Police and Criminal Evidence Act 1984: the role of the Appropriate Adult* (Littlechild,1996).

Experiences of detention
Vulnerable people in detention may feel that what is happening to them is unfair and unjust, and they are being picked upon and harassed. They sometimes may not be clear whether they have done something wrong ,and worry about the outcome. Young people in particular may play the 'hard lad' or 'hard girl' role where they appear not to care and be dismissive of the authoritarian processes going on around them. They may just feel frightened. Vulnerable adults may be confused, be unable to fully comprehend the situation and its consequences, or be afraid of their family's responses and/or those in their informal and formal networks (for example, professionals with whom they have contact).

There is the possibility that the vulnerable person may be overwhelmed by the situation and they may do or say virtually anything to facilitate their release from the police station. They may not bear in mind the possible consequences of what they say, or of their actions, as they often think that any court appearance will be a long time in the future, and this can be worried about later.

It can feel as though the police have a monopoly of power in the situation, and this can lead to a great deal of nervousness and disempowerment for the vulnerable person, and the Appropriate Adult also (see Chapters 4, 6, 9 and 11). These experiences can lead to a suspect making statements or being inadvertently led to say something they do not mean to say, and being intimidated by the situation, even if their immediate presentation to others does not always indicate this. The effect, and types of questioning practices which can be deployed in ways which can seriously disadvantage vulnerable detainees, are revealed in the research of Pearse and Gudjonsson (1999).

Detainees may be desperately trying to maintain both their image and self-image, and concealing nervousness or feelings of intimidation then becomes an important part of that front. Images of how vulnerable people are experiencing their detention might not always be the reality of the situation. It may be that sometimes multiple vulnerability is not always recognised, such as when a young person has a mental health problem or a learning disability; the categories may well be seen as mutually exclusive. No mention is made of the vulnerabilities overlapping in the Codes or in most training concerning this problem, meaning that the effect of multiple vulnerabilities can be missed.

It is important to consider how vulnerable people might experience the Appropriate Adult. This is covered in detail in Chapters 4, 6 and 8, which examine detainees' experiences, and Chapter 11, which addresses Appropriate Adults' views of the important elements of their role. One key area, which was highlighted by both the people who had been detained and contributed to this book and the Appropriate Adults, was the importance of feeling certain that the Appropriate Adult was attending to secure their well being and rights. This was recognised by a number of custody officers as being of importance in Blackie's study (Blackie, 1995).

Who should be called as an Appropriate Adult?
The police are advised in the Codes that they should attempt to call, in order of preference, the following people. For a young person under 17 years of age:

- parent or guardian
- social worker
- another responsible adult who is not employed by the police
  (Code of Practice C, paragraph 1.7 (a))

For a person with mental health or learning disability (or mental handicap, the term the Home Office still insist on using in the Codes), it is slightly different:

- relative, guardian or other person responsible for his or her care or custody
- someone who has experience with mentally disordered or mentally handicapped persons, but is not a police officer employed by the police (such as a approved social worker as defined in the Mental Health Act 1983, or a specialist social worker)

- another responsible adult who is not employed by the police (Code of Practice C, paragraph 1.7 (b))

In a study of custody officers' implementation of the guidelines, Blackie (1995) found that most were aware of the preference list, and the problems with the use of inappropriate Appropriate Adults. A number were concerned to ensure they had secured the most appropriate Appropriate Adult for two reasons: first, to meet the welfare needs of detainees, and second, in order to minimise the risk of any prosecution failing.

For vulnerable adults, a number of police stations in Blackie's study made use of health professionals from local hospitals and community services, as they saw the need for the Appropriate Adult to have knowledge of the detainee's particular circumstances. Neither resourcing nor quality assurance was considered when Codes were enacted (Pearse and Gudjonsson, 1996). Who would these Appropriate Adults be if relatives could not or would not attend? Who would pay for them to be provided?

The great majority of those called have no knowledge of the role, or of its purpose, and can feel as disempowered and intimidated as the vulnerable person. Research carried out for the Royal Commission on Criminal Justice (Runciman, 1993) clearly identified this as a problem; relatives and social workers were shown to be unaware of their role in relation to detained juveniles in the majority of cases, and many relatives of the young people actively undermined the purpose of their presence (see Chapter 9).

Appropriate adults, solicitors and confidentiality
The issue of the relationship between the solicitor and social worker, and how the detainee is made to understand this and make use of it, still raises a number of concerns, particularly as the quality of legal advice has sometimes been queried. Appropriate adults can call the solicitor themselves, overriding the suspect's views, although they should discuss this with the suspect fully before calling a solicitor on their behalf.

A study by Brown (1997) found that the proportion of suspects requesting legal advice has continued to rise since PACE was introduced, and currently is around 38 per cent. Increasing awareness both of the right to legal advice and that advice is free explains some of the increase. Hardly any requests were found to be formally delayed.

However, demand varied considerably between stations and the way in which the right is conveyed by custody officers may account for some of this fluctuation. Of those who request advice, around 80 per cent receive it. The remainder of requests are cancelled or not taken forward for various reasons. Some of the concerns Brown mentions are that in around one-third of legal advice cases advice is given by telephone only; much advice is given by solicitors representatives rather than qualified solicitors; pre-interview consultations with officers are usually brief; and during interviews advisers seldom intervene even where questioning is oppressive, as found in the case of *R. v. Miller, Parris and Abdullah* in 1993 (Cr. App. Review 99). In this case the Lord Chief Justice complained of hostile and intimidating approaches by the police, despite a solicitor's presence. McConville and Hodgson's study (1993) raises grave concerns about the efficacy and value of a good deal of the legal advice given to the police detainees.

The private interview between the Appropriate Adult, the solicitor and the detainee assumes particular importance following a case where a suspect with a mental health problem told his solicitor and social worker in a joint interview that he had carried out a murder. The social worker consulted with his employer and was told to tell the police of this. The solicitor was very aggrieved about this action and there were many repercussions. One of the things that resulted from this was a new element within Law Society's Guide for Solicitors (S.10.1.4b), to the effect that the first consultation with the suspect should take place separately from the Appropriate Adult. Thereafter, the position should be re-assessed as necessary with the suspect being advised of the possibility of disclosure by the Appropriate Adult. This is an area Appropriate Adults should address when setting up the relationship with the detainee to ensure that detainees understand the potential and limitations of the role which the Appropriate Adult is carrying out.

In order to achieve this, Appropriate Adults should make use of the power provided by the Codes to have a private conversation with their client both at the beginning and during the interview if necessary. This is so even if they know the detainee already; the purpose is not to ask about the offence, but to tell the detainee the purpose of their presence, and state that they should not know whether they are guilty or not. Indeed, for professionals, this can cause particular problems; they should not know as it could provide problems because of their codes of ethics. For social workers, for example, though not binding, the code states that:

> *[The social worker] respects the privacy of clients and confidential information about clients gained in his/her relationship with them or others. He or she will divulge confidential information only exceptionally*

where there is clear evidence of serious danger to the client/worker or other persons in the community. (British Association of Social Workers, Code of Ethics)

Other professions also have to consider this issue. This can mean that if someone tells the Appropriate Adult about abuse of others, or a serious offence, this information will have to be passed on to others without the consent of the suspect. It is important that the Appropriate Adult lets other, and most importantly, the suspect, know this. This matter also needs to be made clear in terms of policies and procedures for volunteers or paid sessional workers who act as part of Appropriate Adult schemes.

The Appropriate Adult's interventions

Most vulnerable people will almost certainly have little or no idea about the role of Appropriate Adults in interviews, apart from the streetwise (or police station-wise) learning which some vulnerable people who have been held previously may have gained. Even if they have had an Appropriate Adult before this will not necessarily mean that they will know what they should expect from them, as many Appropriate Adults exhibit a poor level of performance (Evans, 1993a, 1993b). Thus there may be a situation where the vulnerable person might be trying to understand what is happening, as might an Appropriate Adult who is also unsure of their purpose (Littlechild, 1995).

Some Appropriate Adults can be quite aggressive towards the police (Brown, 1997), but in the main it is the case that people do not feel confident to contribute and carry out their role effectively because they feel intimidated within the physical and cultural setting of the police station (Evans, 1993a, 1993b). Therefore it becomes important that Appropriate Adults are prepared in a way that helps them to perform their tasks properly. This is also important for the legal process itself because if there are queries about the Appropriate Adult acting inappropriately, the case may not be taken forward as it should be. For example, if a vulnerable person is guilty of an offence but the Codes have been broken to a significant extent, it can be that the evidence will be deemed inadmissible. If this is the case, guilty people are not going through the full criminal justice process as perhaps they should.

One important issue concerning communication is to make sure that the Appropriate Adult and detainee understand the effects within the criminal justice process of certain answers and ways of questioning. One example is where several people have been arrested in a car, which is suspected of having been stolen. One of the detainees who had not been driving was asked at the time of the interview whether they knew that the car was stolen. The answer was

'Yes', but really the question should have been was he aware at the time that they were in it, that the car was stolen, because subsequent to getting into the car and after the arrest, the police told the detainee that that was why they had been arrested; they might not have known it was stolen at the time they got into the car. It is also important to ensure that detainees understand their rights: Brown *et al.* (1993) found that some detainees did not even receive the Notice to Detained Persons (which is not set in language easy to understand for vulnerable detainees in any event) even though they had signed the custody record to state that they had.

Case law and Appropriate Adults

It is not always easy to base decisions and actions upon case law in a particular situation. It can, though, give guidance on such actions and aid in training and police development. Some decisions, which give an indication of courts' expectations, are set out below. A number of other areas of case law that have particular relevance to young people are also presented in Chapter 9.

In *R. v. Morse* (1991) (Criminal Law Review 195), the judge found that an Appropriate Adult who is unable to discharge any or all of the duties attributable to the role is not an appropriate choice, and puts the interviewee at a disadvantage.

In *R. v. Foster* (1987) (LR 821), the judge excluded evidence under s.78 of PACE for breach of the Codes, stating that it did not matter if such breaches were wilful or ignorant on part of the police. The detainee was subject to four interrogations. However, Lord Lane in *R. v. Delaney* (*The Times,* 3 August 1988) stated that breaches of the Codes do not necessarily invalidate evidence gained from the detention/interview: this depends on the type and severity of the breaches. S.78 of PACE states that interview evidence can be excluded on grounds of unfairness, and Appropriate Adults can be called to give evidence in court.

R. v. Aspinall (*The Times*, 4 February 1999) involved a situation in which the detainee informed the custody officer he suffered from schizophrenia; the Forensic Medical Examiner who attended said that as the detainee was lucid at the time, he was fit to be interviewed, even though he was taking anti-psychotic drugs. He had been in detention for thirteen hours, and was then asked if he wanted a solicitor or any one else present; he said he was anxious and wanted to go home, so refused. The Court of Appeal held that the detention had been in breach of the Codes of Practice, and so the resulting interview was flawed and inadmissible, and the trial judge had been wrong to allow it to be submitted, ignoring the wide range of Appropriate Adult's duties.

David McKenzie had an IQ in the lowest 5 per cent of the population. He was questioned in 1986 concerning arson in an empty flat on his housing estate, which he admitted. He was then questioned about twelve murders, and admitted to them all. Later, in Rampton, where he was held post-conviction, a clinical psychologist presented him with fabricated murders to which David also admitted. David had been told when originally held by the police to 'come clean, and you won't have to go to court', and told no solicitor was available. He was told what to tell them the following day in the interview. No Appropriate Adult was called or was present, and neither was there a solicitor. He was released in November 1992 when the Appeal Court found the original conditions of detention and interviewing unsound.

Stefan Kiszko was convicted of the rape of an 11-year-old girl. He had a low IQ. He spent sixteen years in custody, based on a conviction relying on confession evidence alone. It was later found that police had suppressed evidence. He was acquitted and released by the Court of Appeal.

Issues of fairness and 'oppression' – specifically prohibited in the Codes – in interviews are illustrated in the case of *R. v. Dunn* (3 March 1990, *Times Law Review*). The detainee was convicted of aggravated burglary. No contemporaneous notes were made of the alleged admission and no reason given in the police officer's notebook for this. The detainee had no opportunity to read the subsequent record and sign it. There was a breach of the Codes and s.78: the appeal held that the 'circumstances under which evidence was obtained... [meant] the admission of the evidence would have such an adverse effect on the fairness of the proceedings that the court ought not to admit it'; so 'oppression' was held to have occurred. As a solicitor's clerk (legal executive) was in attendance this tipped the balance in the court's considerations.

A way forward?
The problems set out here have resulted in requirements being brought by Government to provide Appropriate Adult services for juveniles as outlined at the beginning of this chapter. However, there are no suggestions as to how all of these problems would be overcome by a duty being imposed on local authorities who would receive no extra resources to provide these services, welcome though this first step is. There are no new central government resources for social workers' or other professionals' time to service such a scheme. One answer may lie in locally organised Appropriate Adult schemes, combining the use of social workers with volunteers or paid sessional workers, as set out in this book.

An early example of such schemes was in the early 1990s when the Metropolitan Police worked closely with the London Borough of Barnet to set up an Appropriate Adult scheme in order to overcome some of these difficulties (Smith, 1998).

The Borough set up the scheme within the Chief Executive's Department, which developed the scheme in conjunction with Social Services staff. Trained volunteers undertook to be on call for a number of sessions, with 24-hour cover. They undertook to keep their work confidential and attend regular meetings where their needs, and difficulties with the scheme or police, could be discussed. Volunteers have also received refresher training. Such a system, where the focus is on the Appropriate Adult role, is better than most social workers and other professionals can boast. The scheme has been proved successful by an independent evaluation carried out by the Revolving Doors Agency, and it received a favourable mention in a report by Her Majesty's Inspector of Constabulary (1997).

The important elements in setting up and maintaining a successful scheme for adults, as provided by Southampton and New Forest MIND, are described in Chapter 12.

The problem is that such schemes can create bad practice where the support and training provided in these (and the NCH Action for Children scheme for juveniles referred to in Chapter 11) is not in place. It can be that poorly prepared lay people, with minimal (if any) understanding of the role, limited understanding of the needs and difficulties of the person they are supposed to be there for, are disadvantaging vulnerable people further. Worse, they may actually be prejudiced against young people, minority ethnic groups, or people with learning disabilities or mental health problems. They may see themselves as being there to help the police. All these issues would need to be addressed in any scheme, so that it is not a cheap marginalised service that compounds the problems we know already exist in the present arrangements.

In terms of the training and knowledge which needs to be given to Appropriate Adults, there are issues to be covered concerning the suspect's likely experience of detention and vulnerabilities in that situation. There is also a need for the Appropriate Adult to be confident in the role, and to be able talk about it with the suspect. Any preparation should include knowledge about vulnerabilities of those detained and how they might be experiencing the detention, and when and how to intervene where necessary. In addition, those so acting may need to consider their experiences of the police and how they react in those types of situation, so that they minimise the effects of any attitudes that make them overly aggressive or overly compliant in carrying out the role.

Any such scheme might operate under a revised PACE Code of Practice which acknowledged that at times an independent Appropriate Adult would be better all round than a relative who exhorts a suspect to confess to a crime inappropriately, or even abuses them physically, as has been known to happen to some young people. Whilst the new government provision (Youth Justice Board, 2000) requires local authorities to provide Appropriate schemes for juvenile detainees, as set out in more detail in Chapter 9, they do not cover vulnerable adults, and the opportunity should be grasped to include the other vulnerable groups as well. This would require protocols on including Approved Social Workers in the scheme, as currently set out in the Codes.

If rigorously managed schemes are developed, such as the two successful schemes in Southampton referred to in this book (see Chapters 11 and 12), supported by trained and knowledgeable Social Services, health, police and social work professionals on Management Committees, vulnerable suspects might be able to look forward to at least a minimum expectation of having an Appropriate Adult who can attend from a scheme reasonably quickly, who is confident in undertaking the role, and who is concerned about the suspect's welfare.

References

Bean, P and Nemitz, T (1994) *Out of Depth and Out of Sight*, London, Mencap.

Blackie, I (1995) *The Identification of Mental Vulnerability in the Police station under the Police and Criminal Evidence Act 1984*, Unpublished MA Dissertation, Norwich, University of East Anglia.

Brown, D, Ellis, T and Larcombe, K (1993) *Changing the Code: police detention under the revised PACE Codes of Practice* Home Office Research Study 129, London, HMSO.

Brown, D (1997) *PACE 10 years on: a review of research* Home Office Research and Statistics Directorate in 1997 in Research Findings No 49, London, HMSO.

Evans, R (1993a) *The Conduct of Police Interviews with Juveniles, Research Study No 8, Royal Commission on Criminal Justice*, London, HMSO.

Evans, R (1993b) 'Getting things taped' *Community Care* 25 November 1993.

Her Majesty's Inspector of Constabulary (1997) *Report on Inspection of No 2 Area (North West)*, London, HMIC.

Home Office (1985) *Police and Criminal Evidence Act 1984 Codes of Practice*, London, HMSO.

Home Office (1991) *Police and Criminal Evidence Act 1984 Codes of Practice (Revised),* London, HMSO.

Home Office (1995) *Police and Criminal Evidence Act 1984 Codes of Practice (B–E)* London, HMSO.

Home Office (1998a) *Draft Circular on the Final Warning Scheme*, London, Home Office.

Home Office (1998b) *Implementation of the Crime and Disorder Act 1998: England and Wales*, London, Home Office.

Littlechild, B (1995) 'Reassessing the role of the "Appropriate adult"'. *Criminal Law Review*, pp 540–45

Littlechild, B (1996) T*he Police and Criminal Evidence Act 1984: The role of the Appropriate Adult*. Birmingham, British Association of Social Workers.

McConville, M and Hodgson, J (1993) 'Criminal Legal advice and the Right to Silence'. Research Study No. 16, [*The Royal Commission on Criminal Justice Report.*] Cmnd 2263, London: HMSO.

Medford, S, Gudjonsson, G and Pearse, J (2000) *The Identification of Persons at Risk in Police Custody*, London, Institute of Psychiatry.

Palmer, C and Hart, M (1996) *A PACE in the right direction?* Sheffield, Institute for the Study of the Legal Profession.

Pearse, J and Gudjonsson, G (1996) 'How appropriate are Appropriate Adults?' *Journal of Forensic Psychiatry*, 7:3, pp 570–80.

Pearse, J and Gudjonsson, G (1999) 'Measuring influential police interviewing tactics: A factor analysis approach'. *Legal and Criminological Psychology*,4, pp 221–38.

Philips, Sir C (1981) *The Royal Commission on Criminal Justice Report* Cmnd 2263, London, HMSO.

Runciman, Viscount (1993) *The Royal Commission on Criminal Justice Report*. Cmnd 2263. London: HMSO.

Smith, A. (1996) *Is Anything Better than Nothing? A collection of papers from a one day conference,* Birmingham, British Association of Social Workers.

Youth Justice Board (2000) *National Standards for Youth Justice* London, Youth Justice Board.

Chapter 3
The Problems Associated with Implementing the Appropriate Adult Safeguard

John Pearse

To my mind the presence of an Appropriate Adult represents the most important contemporary safeguard for juveniles, mentally ill or psychologically vulnerable suspects detained and interviewed by the police. Unfortunately, securing the attendance of an Appropriate Adult at a police station, usually the first point of entry to the criminal justice system in England and Wales, is not without a number of key operational difficulties. These include the lack of initial identification of vulnerability by police, the limited availability and suitability of some Appropriate Adults and questions over the efficacy of their role and function at the police station. This chapter will provide a brief historical introduction charting the formalisation of the safeguard, and examine some of these areas of concern.

Introduction

It is now more than fourteen years since the Appropriate Adult safeguard was formalised in the Codes of Practice (the Codes) that accompany the Police and Criminal Evidence Act 1984, frequently referred to simply as PACE, Home Office, 1985a, 1985b, 1991, 1995). I think it is important, however, that the introduction of PACE is set in a meaningful context. In a quite radical manner PACE introduced into the daily life of the police a structure and accountability in relation to how they investigated crime, how they stopped and searched suspects, and the manner in which they catered for the detention, treatment and questioning of suspects. PACE effectively provided them with the legitimate means by which to acquire evidence prior to depriving a person of their liberty, yet sought to balance these new powers by providing additional safeguards for all suspects. For example, prior to PACE access to a solicitor was very much in the hands of the police, and the likelihood of legal advice diminished almost in proportion to the serious nature of the offence (Softley, 1980; McConville *et al.* 1991). In other words, the more serious the allegation of crime the less chance a person stood of getting legal advice. PACE changed all this. It created the unequivocal right to free legal advice (s.58) and to ensure compliance, it created the necessary organisation and framework to deliver this safeguard with the introduction of the 'Duty Solicitor Scheme' (s.59). As a result, access to legal advice has continued to rise although some variation has been detected across the country (Brown *et al.*, 1993). For example, in our London study we found an attendance rate of 54 per cent at the lower end of the range, and up to 63 per cent at one station (Pearse and Gudjonsson, 1997).

PACE also instituted different working practices. New posts were introduced (custody officer and reviewing officer), forms unique to each suspect had to be created and made accessible (custody record) and strict time limits were imposed for the detention of suspects with referrals to the Magistrate's Court mandatory after 36 hours. The list of changes to police procedure is considerably longer but, in contextual terms, it may now be possible to appreciate the trepidation with which many police officers greeted the arrival of PACE. Since its introduction in January 1986, however, PACE has been fully adopted by police forces all over the country and time appears to have erased these initial concerns, to the extent that the legislation and resultant regimes have been described as 'a model of operational accountability in much of the rest of the world.' (Newburn and Morgan, 1994:148).

That leaves the question, why was PACE introduced? The answer helps to set many of the current issues in a historical context. PACE evolved as a result of the Royal Commission on Criminal Procedure (Philips, 1981), that was set up in the wake of a number of cases which had aroused considerable public disquiet. Perhaps the most influential incident was the 'Confait Case'. In November 1972, three youths were convicted of a number of offences in relation to the death of Maxwell Confait. All three youths (aged 14, 15 and 18 at the time of their arrest) had signed confession statements having been detained and interviewed by the police. These convictions were subsequently quashed by the Court of Appeal, who declared them to be 'unsafe or unsatisfactory' (S.2, Criminal Appeal Act, 1968) after it was discovered that the youths had been questioned in breach of the Judges' Rules (the guidelines then in place) and in a manner inappropriate to their age. These youths were all psychologically vulnerable. One was, as the Codes would have it, mentally handicapped (learning disability) and illiterate, another of borderline intelligence and near illiterate, and the youngest, although apparently of normal intelligence, spoke English as his second language. Despite this, no legal advisers or independent parties were present for crucial periods of interrogation (Gudjonsson, 1992). Such was the public disquiet raised over this case that a Public Inquiry was ordered under the chairmanship of a retired judge, Sir Henry Fisher, (Fisher, 1977). One of the major findings of this inquiry was that many of the parties involved in the legal process did not understand the safeguards in place for vulnerable suspects.

Alongside a rationalisation of police powers, PACE established four main safeguards for detainees. These were:

- the unequivocal right to free legal advice and the creation of a Duty Solicitor Scheme,

- access to doctors and medical treatment for those in need (physical or psychological),

- the audio-taping of all police interviews

- the introduction of the concept of an Appropriate Adult

Given that not all suspects elect to have legal advice, may not require medical attention, and the audio-tape recording of the interview represents an accountable post-interview record, I would argue that the most important contemporary safeguard for psychologically vulnerable suspects is the presence of an Appropriate Adult.

The question of identification

The legislation contains an inherent assumption that identification of vulnerability will take place and in an effort to maximise the opportunity to capture all vulnerable suspects entitled to an Appropriate Adult the Codes provide a quite sweeping instruction, thus:

> '*If an officer has **any suspicion**, or is told in good faith, that a person of any age may be mentally disordered or mentally handicapped, or mentally incapable of understanding the significance of questions put to him or his replies, then that person shall be treated as a mentally disordered or mentally handicapped person for the purposes of this code.*' (Code C, 1.4: p. 26; my emphasis)

What is interesting is that research has found alarmingly low levels of compliance with this guidance note. For example, Williamson (1990) analysed 1,323 tapes of adult suspects' interviews and found only five Appropriate Adults present (0.4 per cent). In Brown, *et al.*'s (1993) observational study out of 10,048 cases only 106 received an Appropriate Adult (1 per cent). Bean and Nemitz (1994) found that out of 19,472 records only 38 Appropriate Adults were called (0.2 per cent) and finally from 2,721 suspects Robertson, *et al.* (1995) encountered only 13 Appropriate Adults (0.5 per cent). Could it be the case that of all the suspects arrested and detained by the police only 1 per cent or less require an Appropriate Adult? An examination of some baseline figures questions this perspective. For example, rates of prevalence in the general population for learning disability are in the region of 2 per cent and mental illness, we are told, will at some stage affect 1 in 5 of the population (Department of Health, 1994). In addition, many convicted offenders are known to be of below average intellectual ability (Eysenck and Gudjonsson, 1989).

These research findings present a rather disturbing picture of the lack of identification by police. However, the studies noted above were observational or retrospective (archival) projects and do not succeed in providing 'hard' data in respect of the vulnerability, or otherwise, of people arrested by police. To address this issue the Metropolitan Police Service and Institute of Psychiatry combined to undertake empirical research for the last Royal Commission on Criminal Justice and sought to establish a baseline figure for those entitled to the services of an Appropriate Adult (Gudjonsson, *et al.* 1993). All volunteers were subjected to a clinical interview and a limited number of psychological measures. It was hypothesised that many intellectually disadvantaged suspects (that is, those with IQ scores below seventy) possess disabilities that are not readily detected without formal testing, even by experienced clinicians. Therefore at the end of the clinical interview (which addressed issues such as occupation, education, medical background, previous convictions, understanding of legal rights, mental state and alcohol or drug use) the clinician made an assessment with regard to the need for an Appropriate Adult. This was then followed by 4 psychological tests examining suggestibility, intelligence, reading, and state and trait anxiety. Trait anxiety relates to how you would normally react in a given situation. People have certain characteristics and there is a general tendency to react in a consistent and particular way (for example, when meeting a friend). On the other hand, state anxiety reflects how you would react in a specific situation (for example, when arrested and detained by the police). A more detailed account is available in Gudjonsson *et al.* 1993: 6–7, 37–8).

Perhaps the most striking finding was the low IQ scores of many of the suspects. In the first place, almost 9 per cent had an IQ score below 70, with about one-third of the sample capable of being classified as intellectually disadvantaged (N = 156). Second, about 20 per cent of the suspects reported a state anxiety level outside the normal range, indicating that for many suspects being detained at a police station is a highly stressful experience. Despite this high anxiety, many suspects were not found to be unduly suggestible. Third, about 7 per cent of the suspects were thought to be suffering from a major mental illness, such as schizophrenia or depression (N = 163).

In many of these cases such a diagnosis might have been missed without the clinical interview. (N = 171). The clinicians estimated that 25 (15 per cent) suspects required an Appropriate Adult but that when the findings of the psychometric tests were taken into account, the figure would be above 20 per cent. An examination of the Full Scale IQ results reveals that there were actually 9 cases where a suspect's IQ was below 70 (and thus likely to be entitled to an Appropriate Adult under PACE) but they were not identified from the clinical interview as being vulnerable. A more realistic figure therefore, amounts to 34 suspects (21 per cent) who were considered vulnerable and in need of an Appropriate Adult in this study. Such findings confirm the belief that, even for experienced clinicians, the identification of vulnerability within the criminal justice system, and in particular the identification of intellectual deficits, is a particularly complex issue.

The results also serve to highlight the difficulties confronting untrained police officers tasked with the identification of psychological vulnerabilities. In terms of police performance in this 1993 study, it was noted that an Appropriate Adult was summoned in 4 per cent of the cases, which is a considerable increase on the studies mentioned above. The most recent study I am aware of in this area is another collaboration between the Metropolitan Police Service and the Institute of Psychiatry. This is a retrospective study where a psychologist examined the custody records from 73 London charging stations for a specified month and carried out structured interviews with key police personnel, such as the custody officer (Medford, *et al.* 2000). An Appropriate Adult was summoned by police in less than 2 per cent of the cases (more than 27,000 custody records were examined) yet documentary evidence was found by the researcher which suggests that an Appropriate Adult should have been summoned in at least 4.6 per cent of the cases. There is still a considerable discrepancy alongside the 21 per cent suggested by Gudjonsson *et al.* (1993). These findings confirm earlier research which suggests that despite evidence of vulnerability (self-report of depression, previous mental illness, taking medication) police officers are not summoning an Appropriate Adult (Bean and Nemitz, 1994; Palmer and Hart, 1996).

This is a very interesting, yet perplexing, finding. What appears to be happening is that custody officers are abrogating their responsibility, in relation to deciding whether or not to call an Appropriate Adult, to police surgeons (now known as Forensic Medical Examiners or FMEs) who have been called to examine the suspect. Therefore, even in cases where a doctor has been called to examine a suspect because the custody officer has concerns over the person's mental state (that is, the necessary *suspicion*), an Appropriate Adult may not be called (Medford *et al.*, 2000). This is in direct contravention of the guidance given at Code C: par. 1.3, as quoted above, and may lead to a court ruling as inadmissible any evidence obtained thereafter. Interestingly, when interviewed about this discrepancy a number of custody officers stated that it was their duty to call the Appropriate Adult, not the Forensic Medical Examiner, and that they would have no hesitation in doing so even if the latter disagreed. To a limited extent there is some evidence of this occurring (Robertson *et al.*, 1995) but the overwhelming research evidence suggests that many vulnerable suspects are not being identified, and are not receiving the additional safeguard of an Appropriate Adult that is their legal entitlement.

In the London area attempts have been made to alleviate part of this problem with the introduction of a form that is read to all suspects on their arrival at the police station, which is designed to place some of the onus of identification on the suspect. Each suspect is informed that there is special help provided for people with reading difficulties, learning disability or those that may have been to a special school, or who have recently been in a psychiatric hospital or who suffer from mental illness. Unfortunately no research or evaluation study has been carried out on the impact of this form since it was first introduced in 1998, but it is clearly an important area and one that warrants further investigation. There is also evidence available that officers are not calling Appropriate Adults because of the difficulties experienced in getting one to the station and the concern over the suitability of some Appropriate Adults (Pearse, 1995).

Availability and suitability
Availability
In terms of availability, Brown *et al.* (1993) in their observational study examined the time taken to contact an Appropriate Adult for juvenile suspects (N = 1,592). Contact time was taken as the time at which an adult agreed to attend. The average wait increased between phases one and two of the study to 2 hours and 23 minutes although this was inflated by some delays of up to sixteen to seventeen hours for an adult just to be contacted. In 3 per cent of the cases the police were unsuccessful in obtaining an Appropriate Adult. Similar figures are also quoted by Bean and Nemitz (1994) who analysed 19,472 custody records and reported a waiting time of 18 hours in one case and an average waiting time of 3 hours before an Appropriate Adult attended the station. In our recent study the average time difference between the suspect and the Appropriate Adults arrival was 4 hours 35 minutes with a range of zero to

21 hours 35 minutes in vulnerable adult cases. For juveniles the average time difference was almost half that of the adults at 2 hours 21 minutes, with a range of 0 to 18 hours 30 minutes (Medford *et al.*, 2000). A cursory examination of these studies suggests that waiting times are actually increasing. This is clearly an unsatisfactory state of affairs. It is highly unlikely that those responsible for drafting the original PACE legislation could have envisaged that such extensive delays would occur (especially having decreed that the first compulsory review would take place after 6 hours, which was the maximum time thought to be necessary for the processing of general, run of the mill prisoners).

Another, more worrying, corollary is the debilitating effect on the health and welfare of mentally vulnerable suspects who have to endure such prolonged periods of police detention, which is recognised as inherently coercive (Irving, 1980; Gudjonsson, 1992). Looking at it from a custody officer's perspective, they are often faced with a moral dilemma of detaining a person pending the arrival of an Appropriate Adult (to read their rights, undertake an interview or charge the person) or releasing them. So why are these intolerable delays occurring? One of the main reasons is the absence of a formal or structured Appropriate Adult network. This is perhaps the greatest weakness surrounding this safeguard. In desperation, it has been known for police officers to resort to a passing member of the public, people producing driving documents, or a nearby hotel porter (Medford *et al*, 2000) and even the police station cleaner (private communication force training officer).

Suitability
In examining the suitability of people called upon to act as an Appropriate Adult it is often helpful to draw a distinction between juvenile and vulnerable adult suspects. Parents tend to dominate the former category although the picture is less clear in adult cases. In juvenile cases, one immediate question is how appropriate are parents to act in this capacity? Can they, for example, provide a detached and independent service? I am aware of a very experienced and qualified individual who has performed the role of Appropriate Adult many times, to the extent that he has established training courses and launched Appropriate Adult schemes. However, when called upon to act as an Appropriate Adult for one of his own children he has candidly admitted to a public audience that he found himself far too emotionally involved and unable to provide a professional and effective service. In many respects the parent – juvenile suspect scenario encapsulates much of the paradox that surrounds this whole area. There is a lot of research evidence that questions

the wisdom of employing a parent as an Appropriate Adult, but who would deny a parent such an opportunity? Gudjonsson (1993) has established that parents are quite likely to resort to bullying tactics and also that some relatives may suffer from a mental disorder to an extent similar to or even greater than the suspect's. Research by Evans (1993) also questions the partisan role of parents, noting that regardless of whether they supported the police or the child, they did so with equal gusto. He concluded that, by and large they leave juveniles exposed and unsupported. When parents contribute to interviews they are as likely to act for the police as for their children (Evans, 1993: p47).

In adult cases research indicates that the person called upon to act as an Appropriate Adult is unlikely to have any experience of their role will have little or no knowledge of the law and is very unlikely to be familiar with, or assertive enough to contend with, the formal and intimidating regime inside a police station (Dixon, *et al.*, 1990; Brown, *et al.*, 1993; Evans, 1993a, 1993b; Littlechild, 1995; Robertson *et al.*, 1995).

The following extract from Robertson *et al.* (1995) demonstrates that regardless of the qualifications and qualities of an individual, the anticipated role of the Appropriate Adult requires considerable knowledge and resilience:

> *All three authors acted in the capacity of Appropriate Adult in interviews. Despite our professional backgrounds and our familiarity with police stations and police procedures, we all felt that we had little idea what was required of us or what we were allowed to do in terms of intervention. It is made clear to Appropriate Adults by the police that they are free to interject and object if they think this is necessary, but we imagine that very few people who act as Appropriate Adults know when it would be appropriate to object and that even fewer would have the courage to interrupt the police in their business of questioning someone.* (Robertson *et al.*, 1995:69)

My own research has highlighted the difficulties facing Appropriate Adults, especially in high profile cases, who have been called upon to act as an independent safeguard without sufficient training or experience. Another major impediment that impacts on the question of suitability concerns the poorly defined role of the Appropriate Adult, as outlined in the Codes.

Performing the role of the Appropriate Adult
Given the absence of a recognised framework for the recruitment and training of Appropriate Adults it is highly likely that prospective Appropriate

Adults will need to seek advice on their arrival at a police station. The official version contained in the Codes is not required to be delivered by the police until the start of the police interview, even though this may be a considerable time after the suspect's or Appropriate Adult's arrival at the station.

According to the Codes, the official role is as follows:

> *Where an Appropriate Adult is present at an interview, he should be informed that he is not expected to act simply as an observer; and also that the purposes of his presence are, first, to advise the person being questioned and to observe whether or not the interview is being conducted properly and fairly, and secondly, to facilitate communication with the person being interviewed.* (Code C, 1991: 55)

Some indication of an 'unofficial' version (provided by an officer in response to an enquiry from a social worker) was noted by Dixon *et al.*, (1990:120): 'You are wallpaper, pal'.

The official advice envisages an active rather than a passive role in terms of 'what' the Appropriate Adult should do but what is not clear is exactly what advice should be given? Should an Appropriate Adult provide legal advice or, indeed, advice that overrides legal advice? According to one legal source, the role includes: 'advising the suspect about a number of crucial decisions that have to be made while at the police station, such as when to remain silent and refuse to answer police questions' (Rhead, 1997). This interpretation by Rhead (a criminal solicitor and visiting university lecturer) suggests that the Appropriate Adult can indeed provide legal advice, even though this is totally contrary to the spirit and letter of PACE. At the moment the wording of the advice in the Codes can be interpreted as being designed to propel the roles of the solicitor and Appropriate Adult into direct conflict. This is exactly what happened in one case where a suspect had been arrested for murder and had been advised by his solicitor not to answer police questions. The Appropriate Adult, however, in a bid to 'facilitate communication', encouraged the suspect to provide his version of events and due to this conflict the solicitor succeeded in having the Appropriate Adult removed from the interview (Pearse, 1997).

In another example, a psychologist was called to act as an Appropriate Adult and to assess a man arrested for murder, whose behaviour the police had described as 'very odd'. The solicitor acting for the suspect refused the Appropriate Adult permission to see his client on the grounds that he had been called in by the police and that anything his client might say to him as an

Appropriate Adult would not be confidential. In interview the suspect exhibited very idiosyncratic behaviour but without the benefit of a prior assessment the Appropriate Adult was unable to interpret the symptoms accurately (Pearse and Gudjonsson, 1996). What was the Appropriate Adult to do? This case serves as a practical example where it was not possible for the Appropriate Adult to 'advise the person', or effectively 'observe' the fairness of proceedings, or indeed 'facilitate communication'. His role as an Appropriate Adult was redundant and his participation reduced to that of an observer, even though 'he shall be informed that he is not expected to act simply as an observer' (Code C, 1995: 55).

To date quantitative research has dominated this area. We are aware of the poor levels of identification that are taking place, the limited number of Appropriate Adults attending stations and the extensive delays experienced in waiting for the arrival of an Appropriate Adult. We are not so well informed in relation to what the Appropriate Adult actually does in the interview. In other words, to what extent does the Appropriate Adult perform the role as envisaged within the Codes? My own research has highlighted the passive nature of Appropriate Adults (that is, they tend not to intervene) even in run of the mill cases. What needs to be addressed is whether the action of the Appropriate Adult during the interview was appropriate. By that, I mean did the circumstances of the interview demand that an intervention be made? If so, was an intervention made and was it appropriate? Similarly, if they remained silent was there any evidence that they should have intervened? I examined 172 adult criminal cases and found that an Appropriate Adult was present in 8 (5 per cent) of the cases but that an intervention was made in only half of these examples (Pearse, 1997). Included in this sample of four was one case where the researcher had agreed to act as an Appropriate Adult as no other suitable candidate could be located by the police. With this case removed, an intervention was made in three out of the remaining seven cases.

In all three cases the intervention by the Appropriate Adult was inappropriate. In the first case the suspect dominated and controlled the contribution of the Appropriate Adult, and the Appropriate Adult later provided a very unsatisfactory alibi for the suspect. In the second case another questionable alibi was forthcoming from the Appropriate Adult and in the final case the Appropriate Adult started answering questions for the suspect, which was wholly unnecessary and served only to provide unrealistic scenarios for the interviewing officers to contend with (Pearse, 1997). In the remaining four cases where no intervention was made, three of the cases were very straightforward, brief interviews that did not warrant a contribution from the Appropriate Adult. In the fourth example, however, the interview rapidly degenerated into a shouting and heckling exchange between the officer and the suspect, which failed to produce an intervention from the Appropriate Adult or the solicitor present. Extending this methodology to examples of twenty very serious criminal cases (murder, arson, rape), I found six examples where an Appropriate Adult was present. I was only able to award a satisfactory rating to one of these six cases. In two of the remaining five cases the Appropriate Adults stayed silent when the situation demanded otherwise but, more worryingly, in the remaining three cases, it was actually an intervention, or prompt, from the Appropriate Adult that preceded the confession. Unfortunately the numbers involved in both studies are far too small to allow generalisation to the whole population or to specific types of cases, but they do begin to show an alarming insight into the activities and decision making qualities (or lack of them) of some Appropriate Adults.

Conclusion
The Appropriate Adult has never enjoyed the structure and organisation attached to the provision of a solicitor or a doctor for people detained at police stations, and has suffered accordingly. The Appropriate Adult provision appears in secondary legislation (the Codes) and not in primary legislation (PACE), thus relegating it to an unsatisfactory and often unworkable safeguard. Some of the reasons behind this failure have been discussed in this chapter, but the real irony remains that the genesis of PACE (a radical and progressive statute) evolved because of the inappropriate treatment of vulnerable suspects; yet for now the same legislation still fails to protect the most vulnerable.

We must be careful not to lose sight of the fact that whilst the presence of an Appropriate Adult in adult cases is relatively rare, the actual need for this safeguard appears overrepresented in recent historic Court of Appeal judgements (Gudjonsson, 1992; Corre, 1995). There remains a considerable moral duty on all agencies to highlight and overcome these deficiencies, and this situation may be more robustly addressed by future European legislation than has hitherto been the case.

References
Bean, P and Nemitz, T (1994) *Out of Depth and Out of Sight* London, MENCAP.

Brown, D, Ellis, T and Larcombe, K (1993) *Changing the Code: police detention under the revised PACE codes of practice* London, HMSO.

Corre, N (1995) *The 1995 Revisions to The PACE Codes of Practice* London, Callow.

Department of Health (1994) *Working with Mentally Disordered Offenders: A training pack for social services staff and others dealing with mentally disordered offenders* London, NACRO / Department of Health.

Dixon, D, Bottomley, A, Coleman, C, Gill, M, and Wall, D (1990) 'Safeguarding the rights of suspects in police custody' *Policing and Society* 1:115–40.

Evans, R (1993a) 'The Conduct of Police Interviews with Juveniles' *Research Study No. 8. The Royal Commission on Criminal Justice* London, HMSO.

Evans, R (1993b) 'Getting Things Taped' *Community Care* 19 November.

Eysenck, H J, and Gudjonsson, G H. (1989) *The Causes and Cures of Criminality* New York and London, Plenum Press.

Fisher, H (1977) *Report of an Inquiry by the Hon. Sir Henry Fisher Into the Circumstances Leading to the Trial of Three Persons on Charges Arising out of the Death of Maxwell Confait and the Fire at 27 Doggett Road, London, SE6.* London, HMSO.

Gudjonsson, G H (1992) *The Psychology of Interrogations, Confessions and Testimony* Chichester, John Wiley.

Gudjonsson, G H (1993) 'Confession evidence, Psychological vulnerability and expert testimony' *Journal of Community and Applied Social Psychology* 3, pp 117–29.

Gudjonsson, G H, Clare, I C H, Rutter, S and Pearse, J (1993) 'Persons at Risk During Interviews in Police Custody: The Identification of Vulnerabilities Research Study No. 12' *The Royal Commission on Criminal Justice* London, HMSO.

Home Office (1985a) *The Police and Criminal Evidence Act 1984* London., HMSO.

Home Office (1985b) *The Police and Criminal Evidence Act 1984 (s.66) Codes of Practice* London., HMSO.

Home Office (1991) *The Police and Criminal Evidence Act 1984 (s.66) Codes of Practice, Revised edition* London., HMSO.

Home Office (1995) *The Police and Criminal Evidence Act 1984 (s.66) Codes of Practice B–E,* London., HMSO.

Irving, B (1980) *Police Interrogation. A Case Study of Current Practice. Research Study No. 2* London., HMSO.

Littlechild, B (1995) 'Reassessing the Role of the 'Appropriate Adult' *Criminal Law Review* 540–5.

McConville, M, Sanders, A and Leng, R (1991) *The Case for the Prosecution: Police Suspects and the Construction of Criminality* London, Routledge.

Medford, S, Gudjonsson, G H and Pearse, J (2000) *The Identification of Persons at Risk in Police Custody: the use of Appropriate Adults by the Metropolitan Police* London, Metropolitan Police Service, May.

Newburn, T and Morgan, R (1994) 'A new agenda for the old Bill?' *Policing* 10 (.3), pp 143–50.

Palmer, C and Hart, M (1996) *A PACE in the right direction?* Sheffield Institute for the Study of the Legal Profession, University of Sheffield.

Pearse, J (1995) 'Police Interviewing: The Identification of Vulnerabilities'. *The Journal of Community and Applied Social Psychology* (5), 147–59.

Pearse, J (1997). 'Police interviewing: An examination of some of the psychological, interrogative and background factors that are associated with a suspect's confession' Unpublished PhD Thesis, Institute of Psychiatry, University of London.

Pearse, J and Gudjonsson, G H (1996) 'How Appropriate are Appropriate Adults?' *Journal of Forensic Psychiatry* 7(3) pp 570–80.

Pearse, J and Gudjonsson, G H (1997) Police interviewing and legal representation: a field study. *Journal of Forensic Psychiatry*, 8 (10), 200 -208.

Philips, Sir C (1981) *The Royal Commission on Criminal Procedure Report* Cmnd 8092, London, HMSO.

Rhead, A (1997) 'Safely in to dock?' *Community Care*, 13–19.March.

Robertson, G, Pearson, R and Gibb, R (1995) *The Entry of Mentally Disordered People to the Criminal Justice System* Home Office Research and Statistics Department, Research Findings No.21, London, Home Office.

Softley, P assisted by Brown, D, Forde, B, Mair, G and Moxon, D (1980) *Police Interrogation: an observational study in four police stations* London, HMSO.

Williamson, T M (1990) 'Strategic Changes In Police Interrogation: An Examination of Police and Suspect Behaviour in the Metropolitan Police in Order to Determine the Effects of New Legislation, Technology and Organisational Policies' Unpublished PhD Thesis, University of Kent.

Chapter 4
Mental Health Problems: One person's use

Grethe Hansen

Research has examined Appropriate Adult schemes from the perspective of the police (Pearse, 1995; Evans and Rawstorne, 1997) and of the Appropriate Adult (Thomas, 1995). The psychological characteristics and mental health of suspects have also been investigated in research (Gudjonsson *et al.*, 1993). Very little attention has focused on the actual experience of detention by people with mental health problems, a crucial perspective which is now increasingly recognised as a significant outcome measure in any service evaluation (see, for instance, Department of Health, 1999) and a perspective without which any discussion of the Appropriate Adult service would be incomplete.

This chapter is based on a discussion with a mental health service user, Mike (not his real name), who has been detained by the police numerous times. Mike was asked to discuss his own experiences only and his views do not necessarily represent the views of other people with mental health problems. However, Mike gives a vivid account of being in custody and the interview may therefore provide some pointers to future research into Appropriate Adult schemes, focusing on the experiences of people with mental health problems.

Mike, a white man in his late forties, lives in a town in Southern England. I met Mike through the local mental health service. Prior to the interview I had asked for no information about Mike's personal history and been given no details about his current or past mental health problems, or the reasons for his police detentions as this was considered irrelevant to the purpose of the interview: the experience of being detained in police custody and of the Appropriate Adult service. At Mike's request his mental health worker was present during the interview, which took place in his home.

Mike explains that he has been arrested by the police frequently over the last 30 years. His general observations about being detained and spending time at a police station are:

> *'It's very intimidating in a police station and as I say I've been going in there years, it's very intimidating. It is very, very daunting. You never get used to it, well, I've never got used to it.*

'*I mean you can be in a police station where you can get railroaded, it does happen. You have got good police officers – there are also bad ones as well. But you do get railroaded sometimes into admitting things. Sometimes if you're in a police station, if you're on your own, they will tend to keep you for as long as they can keep you, you know 24 hours, before they have to get extra time. Then they start firing questions at you – and it's 'Oh! well go on then, I must have done it.' It just sounds familiar, so you admit it. I've got quite an extensive record and nine times out of ten I admit what I've done, whether I've done it or not – then change my mind afterwards. To be quite honest, that's what I do. Then I plead not guilty.*

'*Nine times out of ten when I was arrested it was more for drink related, or something like that. The trouble is when I'm in a police station I've had a lot to drink, or if I'm feeling unwell myself, then I tend to agree to anything. I tend to agree to get out and get it all over with, even if I haven't done it sometimes I agree to it. They will leave you in a cell for 4 or 5 hours to sober up and then you just want a drink, so then they question you and you're going to admit to anything. Just to get out of there. Especially if it's nine o'clock at night you just want to get out and have a pint.*'

The PACE Codes of Practice (Home Office 1995) states:

It is important to bear in mind that, although juveniles or people who are mentally disordered or mentally handicapped are often capable of providing reliable evidence, they may, without knowing or wishing to do so, be particularly prone in certain circumstances to provide information which is unreliable, misleading or self-incriminating. Special care should therefore always be exercised in questioning such a person, and the appropriate adult should be involved, if there is any doubt about a person's age, mental state or capacity. Because of the risk of unreliable evidence it is also important to obtain corroboration of any facts admitted whenever possible. (Code C, Notes for Guidance 11B, p. 56)

It is clear from Mike's description of his numerous detentions that he considers himself 'particularly prone in certain circumstances to provide information which is unreliable, misleading or self-incriminating'. This may be attributed to mental health problems, though Mike appears to link it to a desire get released before the pubs close.

Gudjonsson *et al.* (1993) investigated the psychological characteristics of all adult suspects in two Metropolitan Police stations over a three-month period in order to gauge the need for the Appropriate Adult service. The researchers use a very wide definition of vulnerability and found that between 15 and 20 per cent of all suspects were suffering from mental health problems, taking into account psychological factors, such as suggestibility (Gudjonsson *et al.*, 1993). It is clear from Mike description that he could be described as highly suggestible when in police custody, regardless of the cause of this suggestibility.

Since the mid-1990s Mike has usually had an Appropriate Adult present when in custody. Mike is extremely positive about this service and many of the perceived benefits he has experienced are those intended by the PACE Codes of Practice (Home Office, 1995):

> *Where the appropriate adult is present at an interview, he shall be informed that he is not expected to act simply as an observer; and also that the purpose of his presence are, first, to advise the person being questioned and to observe whether or not the interview is being conducted properly and fairly, and secondly, to facilitate communication with the person being interviewed.* (Code C, 11.16)

Mike finds the presence of an Appropriate Adult very useful in counteracting the intimidating experience of being in custody and finds that this stops him confessing to crimes he has not committed:

> *I think that you feel that you're not alone, because in there it's very daunting, you're on your own with one or two police officers and they fire questions at you and things like that. Whereas if the appropriate adult is there it sorts of helps me to sort it out and there's someone there to talk it over with and things like that. Because I just want to get out of there half the time, I end up saying anything. Whereas the appropriate adult more or less doesn't let me say what I want to say and she's there so obviously the police do tend to hurry up anyway. They don't take the advantages they would take with me on my own. Not all police are like that – some of them are pretty good.*

Mike also recounts that an Appropriate Adult will ensure that he is given the rights to which he is entitled according to PACE:

> *Medication and things like that, to make sure that I've seen a doctor. I think I had one appropriate adult who came in and said how long have I been here and why haven't I got any food? Do you want a solicitor here?*

I found that also it, with the appropriate adult there, the police were more intent to put you on police bail, to come back in a week or a month's time. The appropriate adult will get you out a lot quicker anyway, out of the police station. It's very intimidating in a police station.

Mike and the Appropriate Adult always meet on their own, as stipulated in the Code of Practice (Code C, paragraph 3.12).

Mike remembers the first time he had an Appropriate Adult present: 'The sergeant who was there then he said: "I think you've got to have someone here". So they brought someone in and actually I knew them. It was someone I knew who turned up.'

The term Appropriate Adult did not initially convey any meaning for Mike and he still finds the term strange and inappropriate: 'You think it's for children, to be honest.'

The Code of Practice defines an Appropriate Adult as:

(a)   *a relative, guardian or some other person responsible for his care or custody;*

(b)   *someone who has experience of dealing with mentally disordered or mentally handicapped people but not a police officer or employed by the police; or*

(c)   *failing either of the above, some other responsible adult aged 18 or over who is not a police officer or employed by the police.*
      (Code C, Annex E, paragraph 2)

The Notes of Guidance further recommend:

'In the case of mentally disordered or mentally handicapped people, it may in certain circumstances be more satisfactory for all concerned if the appropriate adult is someone who has experience or training in their care rather than a relative lacking such qualifications. But if the person himself prefers a relative to a better qualified stranger or objects to a particular person as the appropriate adult, his wishes should if practicable be respected.' (Code C, Notes of Guidance E1)

Mike was not aware of this provision and has never been given a choice of Appropriate Adult. When he is detained he always has a member of the local mental health team and reports: ' You get whose on duty, I think. I've been lucky every time I've had someone I know.' Mike has no relatives living locally.

As mentioned by Mike above, the Appropriate Adults who are present during Mike's detentions always ask if he wishes a solicitor present. Mike invariably declines. It would appear that the Appropriate Adults never find it necessary to ask a solicitor regardless of Mike's wishes, though the Code makes this possible: 'If, having been informed of the right to legal advice ... either the appropriate adult or the person detained wishes legal advice to be taken, then the provision of section 6 of this code apply' (Code C, paragraph 3.13).

Mike has some interesting observations about the differences between the role of a solicitor and of an Appropriate Adult:

The solicitor will just tell you to say nothing. Don't say anything. But I always find if there's someone else there with you then the police won't get up to certain things that they get up to, like keep on and on questioning you.

The problem you have with solicitors is they can't always come out when you want them like. So it could be 4 or 5 or 6 hours before a solicitor comes out, so you're stuck in the cell all that time.

The solicitor won't always come out, especially if you've had a drink or something like that. Or if it's a minor charge or anything like that. Because they know you're going to get bailed anyway so what's the point of them coming out.

I always found that the appropriate adult sort of acts like a solicitor anyway, so I didn't really need a solicitor. I didn't need both of them there. Whereas the appropriate adult more or less come out straight away, more or less.

There has never been any problems in terms of long delays in waiting for somebody. With solicitors there is.

The promptness in the attendance of Appropriate Adults is unusual according to several pieces of research into Appropriate Adult schemes (Pearse, 1995; Evans and Rawstorne, 1997) and is a credit to the local mental health services and to the working relationship between those services and the police.

When asked to contrast the experiences of being in custody with and without an Appropriate Adult Mike responds: 'I always got charged when there was no appropriate adult.'

The Code of Practice makes it very clear that where a Custody Sergeant has any doubt as to the mental state or capacity of a person detained an appropriate adult should be called. (Code C, Notes of Guidance 1G).

37

However, as can be seen from the following, Mike's experiences with the police have led him to develop some interesting notions about the circumstances which require the presence of an Appropriate Adult. When asked about the detentions in the last few years when an Appropriate Adult had not been present Mike replies:

The last time was about 3 years ago. I think it's just that the charge was too serious and I got caught red-handed anyway. It's not only that – I was sober as well – I suppose that's what it was. I was three parts sober, I'd had a drink but was not drunk.

Asked if he had felt the need for an Appropriate Adult at that time Mike answers:

No. I'm going to be fair with the police on this one – I mean I got caught banged to rights, to be honest, they got me in and out as quick as possible. I stuck my hand up.

Sometimes when I'm feeling really down, I go out and do something, I mean we always talked about committing criminal suicide. It's like you're deliberately trying to get caught. I do something in front of someone. Sometimes I even phone the police up and tell them that I'm going to do it. Sometimes, when I've had a bit to drink, or if I'm feeling depressed or something like that, I feel that I need an appropriate adult. As I say some sergeants down there will see that and contact an appropriate adult.

However, custody sergeants vary in their requests for an Appropriate Adult:

Although I'm down for an appropriate adult whenever I go in there it just doesn't always come about. Some sergeants will say right, you need an appropriate adult, others will not say that. So if I don't ask for an appropriate adult, you won't get one. Some sergeants are good down there. There was one time there when I went a bit potty in the police station, I mean I was whacking my head against the wall, and then he said 'I think you've got to have an appropriate adult.'

It's like a lot of my offences now I don't get charged for, they put me in front of a mental health panel, or something. Obviously if it's something serious then they've got to charge me, but if it's something like being drunk or something like theft, they don't necessarily charge me no more.

It's very, very intimidating. If you are down for an appropriate adult, or if you're down as mentally unstable, whatever, under the Mental Health Act, they should automatically insist on an appropriate adult. I think so. But it does not always happen.

According to Mike's experience an Appropriate Adult should be present if someone is drunk or mentally unstable at the time of the arrest ('criminal suicide','deliberately trying to get caught' or 'down or depressed') and when someone is on record as needing an Appropriate Adult. He also appears to link the presence of an Appropriate Adult with not being charged for an offence. However, if the offence is serious and the suspect is 'caught red-handed' he feels an Appropriate Adult is unnecessary, which is perhaps not surprising given Mike's tendency to admit to various crimes with which he has no involvement.

The worrying aspect of Mike's experience is the apparent inconsistency of custody sergeants: in spite of being on the police records as someone with a mental health problem to whom an Appropriate Adult should be called Mike himself does not feel he can rely on the police and at times has to make the request himself. Given the police's concern about inadmissible evidence it is surprising that the local force – according to Mike's account – appear to repeatedly allow Mike to make self-incriminating and unsubstantiated confessions in his efforts to get released, only to retract these statements at a later date.

The above discussion led to the final part of the interview: what advice would Mike give to the police about the Appropriate Adult service and to Appropriate Adults themselves?

I think they should be more aware – to certain categories of people. They've got me appropriate adults before so it should be done nearly every time you go in, well every time. They have had to section me and I think, now they've got that on file anyway, so I think they should automatically say: appropriate adult, which they don't do. I have to ask for an appropriate adult, so if I didn't know about the appropriate adult now, then I probably wouldn't get one.

They have computers now, they've all your records. As I say by them sectioning me a couple [of] times obviously they know all about it, all about my problems and they have had to come back here and get my tablets sometimes when they have got to keep me in. They've took me in for me own safety, I must admit. A little while ago I've smashed all the windows out and the police have come up here, they kicked the door down and said 'well are you liable to do it again' so I said I didn't know. So they took me in and gave me a lift home in the morning, so I can't, you know, so the police are not all bad.

If I get arrested like I am now, which never happens because whenever I'm sober and sensible I never get arrested because I don't do anything. I think they should give you the opportunity or at least inform someone or other which they don't.

In the above Mike is agreeing with Pearse (1995) who, when discussing the importance of internal police communication, recommends:

> *Files in relation to individuals known to require the presence of an Appropriate Adult should be marked accordingly. The Police National Computer (PNC), which contains information relating to convicted offenders, provides a system of warning signals immediately available to all officers.* (Pearse, 1995: 156)

Mike only ever discussed arrests in one town and yet it appears that the information about Mike's mental health problems and usual behaviour when detained is not shared among the officers within that one police station.

Finally here is Mike's advice for Appropriate Adults: 'To listen, and to look up on the rules, I suppose. Stick with them, stick by their side. Because that's the bit, it's very intimidating in a police station and as I say I've been going in there years.'

Comments

It is clear that being in a police station is a very daunting experience for Mike, even after thirty years. Mike greatly values the service of an Appropriate Adult. He appreciates the speed with which they attend, and their presence stops him making false admissions and enables him to cope with the intimidation of the police station. He is quite understandably dissatisfied that an Appropriate Adult is not consistently offered to him, particularly when he is drunk or depressed.

Mike's account suggests that there is a good working relationship between the local police and mental health services, as demonstrated by the speed in obtaining an Appropriate Adult. The Appropriate Adult scheme also clearly provides an invaluable service both to Mike and within the criminal justice system. However, the police appear to need to develop their skills in identifying vulnerable people with mental health problems, as well as to improve their communication systems to enable them to respond consistently.

References

Department of Health (1999) *National Service Framework for Mental Health. Modern Standards and Service Models* London, HMSO.

Evans, R and Rawstorne, S (1997) 'Appropriate Behaviour' *Community Care* 17–23 July, pp 30–1.

Gudjonsson, G, Clare, I and Rutter S (1993) 'Persons at risk during interviews in police custody: the identification of vulnerabilities, Research Study No.12' *The Royal Commission on Criminal Justice* London, HMSO.

Home Office (1995): Police and Criminal Evidence Act. 1984 Code of Practice B–E, London, HMSO

Pearse, J (1995) 'Police Interviewing: The Identification of Vulnerabilities' *Journal of Community & Applied Psychology* 5, pp. 1147–59.

Thomas, T (1995) 'The Continuing Story of the "Appropriate adult"' *The Howard Journal* 34(2), May.

Chapter 5
Mental Health Problems:
Recognition and risk

Grethe Hansen

PACE and suspects with mental health problems

Like anyone else, people with mental health problems may have contact with the police in a number of ways: as suspects, as witnesses or as victims of a crime. The 1984 Police and Criminal Evidence Act (PACE) imposes particular duties on the police in relation to adults with mental health problems detained as suspects. (In this chapter I will mainly use the term *people with mental health problems* in preference to the terms *mental illness* and *mental disorder*. *People with mental health problems* is generally more acceptable to people who use mental health services as it emphasises the person and reduces the stigma associated with the words *mental illness* and *mental disorder*.)

This chapter is designed to help custody sergeants, Forensic Medical examiners and others to identify and deal with the difficulties of detainees who may be suffering from a mental health problem and therefore be entitled to the services of an Appropriate Adult.

The PACE Codes of Practice (Home Office, 1995b) state that:

> *If an officer has any suspicion, or is told in good faith, that a person of any age may be mentally disordered or mentally handicapped, or mentally incapable of understanding the significance of questions put to him or his replies, then that person shall be treated as mentally disordered or mentally handicapped for the purposes of this code.* (Code C, Annex E. 1, p. 75)

> *It is important to bear in mind that, although juveniles or people who are mentally disordered or mentally handicapped are often capable of providing reliable evidence, they may, without knowing or wishing to do so, be particularly prone in certain circumstances to provide information which is unreliable, misleading or self-incriminating. Special care should therefore always be exercised in questioning such a person, and the appropriate adult should be involved, if there is any doubt about a person's age, mental state or capacity. Because of the risk of unreliable evidence it is also important to obtain corroboration of any facts admitted whenever possible.* (Code C. Note of Guidance 11B, p. 56)

The provision in the 1984 PACE Act and the Code of Practice is intended both to protect suspects with mental health problems from undue stress whilst being interviewed by the police and to protect the police from obtaining evidence which would prove inadmissible in court. However, as pointed out by Pearse (1995), whilst the Act includes a definition of 'mental handicap' – the term used in the Codes – neither the main body of the Act nor the Code of Practice provide an operational definition of mental disorder or of mental illness. There is an assumption that people with mental health problems are particularly liable to make false confessions or self-incriminating statements; yet many people who do not appear to have mental health problems make false confessions or statements that incriminate them (Pearse, 1995).

A recent ruling by the Court of Appeal raises an interesting question regarding which operational definition the police ought to adopt in relation to suspects with mental health problems. A suspect diagnosed with schizophrenia and taking anti-psychotic drugs was considered by the Forensic Medical Examiner to be lucid and fit to be interviewed. The man was detained for thirteen hours and was then asked if he wanted a solicitor or anyone else present. He declined, saying he was anxious to go home. The Court of Appeal ruled that the detention had been in breach of the Code of Practice (*R.* v. *Aspinall, The Times*, 4 February 1999).

Should someone with a diagnosis of a mental health problem always be assumed to be vulnerable regardless of how long ago this diagnosis was made and regardless of the mental state of the person at the time of the police interview? Many people with mental health problems feel they are forever held to be 'invalid' as regards to all aspects of their life because of the stigma attached to mental health problems (Stanley et al. 1999). Many would deeply resent the assumption that they by definition are prone to make false admissions and in general are less trustworthy than the general population. Having a mental health problem is for many people fortunately a transient experience. Yet many feel that once they have been diagnosed they are prevented from moving on with their lives because the label is so powerful and negative. Having a diagnosis of, and getting treatment for, a severe mental health problem, such as schizophrenia does not mean that someone is in a permanent florid state and will behave and feel abnormally in all situations for the rest of their life.

The 1984 Police and Criminal Evidence Act and the Code of Practice require the police to identify those people who are vulnerable at the time of police interview. The personal history, as well as the actual behaviour at the time, are obviously factors that contribute to such an identification.

However, broad psychiatric categories, possibly applied a considerable time ago, are not helpful to the police without an operational definition which focuses on the actual presenting picture at the time of interview.

Research suggests that the police have difficulties identifying mental health problems in people detained in police stations. Appropriate Adults tend to get called in when a detained person is behaving in a very bizarre manner and is in an obviously florid state. At other times vulnerability due to mental health problems may be undetected and the person does not gain access to an Appropriate Adult (Evans and Rawstorne, 1997). Gudjonsson *et al.*, (1993) investigated the psychological characteristics of all adult suspects in two Metropolitan Police stations over a three-month period. The researchers found that 7 per cent of suspects were suffering from mental health problems, yet the police only arranged the service of an Appropriate Adult in 4 per cent of all interviews, (Gudjonsson *et al.*, 1993). Taking into account psychological factors, such as suggestibility, the researchers found that between 15 and 20 per cent of all suspects should have had an Appropriate Adult present (Home Office, 1995a). This conclusion is based on a wide definition of vulnerability. (For further examination of such research studies, see Chapter 3).

The research raises questions about the appropriate definition of vulnerability in relation to mental health problems, the lack of guidelines for applying the requirements of the Act, and the level of police training in relation to assessment of mental state. The research also suggests that one of the important factors that may determine vulnerability is the difficulty the police report in obtaining an Appropriate Adult. If there are significant problems in obtaining Appropriate Adults the police may ignore suspicions about suspects' vulnerability, thereby possibly denying vulnerable people a service to which they are entitled as well carrying out practice contrary to the PACE Code of Practice (Pearse, 1995)

The absence of clear guidelines and the concern about 'inadmissibility' help neither the police nor people with current or past mental health problems to achieve a balance between the protection of vulnerable adults and the damaging stigma of a diagnosis of mental health problems.

Crime and people with mental health problems

It is a very common perception that everyone with a mental health problem presents an increased risk of violence in most situations. This perception is likely to influence any decision making process, including the judgements made about people in custody who may have a mental health problem.

Police behaviour based on this perception may well contribute to tension and stress for both police and suspects and may in itself increase the risk of aggression or violence. It is therefore crucial to be aware of the statistical evidence regarding crimes committed by people with mental health problems, whilst always treating each suspect according to their own individual history and current mental state and circumstances.

Statistics show no overall correlation between crime and people with mental health problems and the rate for all crimes is no higher than for the general population. For non-violent crime the rate is the same for people with mental health problems as for the general population (Department of Health, 1994).

The link between homicide and people with mental health problems has received a great deal of attention in the last few years, yet the figures do not appear to justify the common perception of rising numbers of homicides committed by people for whom 'community care' has failed: an analysis of statistics in England and Wales from 1957 to 1995 showed a 3 per cent annual decline in homicides by people with a diagnosed mental health problem (Taylor and Gunn, 1999).

In the 1960s nearly 50 per cent of all people convicted of homicide had a diagnosed mental health problem. In the 1990s this figure had fallen: 14 per cent of people convicted of homicide had symptoms of a mental health problem at the time of committing the offence (Appleby *et al.*, 1999). People with mental health problems are less likely to kill a stranger: 10 per cent of victims, compared to 26 per cent of victims in homicides by people without mental health problems. The victims are far more likely to be family members: 82 per cent of victims compared to 25 per cent (Jewesbury *et al.*, 1998).

In fourteen out of seventeen inquiry reports of homicide by people with mental health problems the person had a substance abuse problem. In about 50 per cent of those cases the substance abuse problems were considered to be a major contributory factor in the crime (Ward and Applin, 1998).

Risk and suspects with mental health problems
The links between mental health problems and risk to self and others are very complex. When someone has a mental health problem it does not mean that everything that person does will be different from the way most other people would react, given the circumstances. Behaviour will be influenced not just by psychiatric diagnosis but by a multiplicity of other factors, and everyone must be considered in relation to their individual personality, history and current context.

Risk is not a static concept and broad diagnostic categories are not useful or reliable predictors of risk. It is meaningless to try to predict how likely it is that a person will commit a crime or a violent act, basing the prediction solely on the diagnosis which in any case may have been made a considerable time ago. It is far more meaningful to ask in what circumstances the risk might arise for that particular person.

Inquiry reports into the care of individual people with mental health problems, such as Christopher Clunis, have shown that a key element in risk assessment is information sharing and the crucial factor in risk management is prevention of vulnerability (Reith, 1998).

Guidelines on assessment of risk in relation to people with mental health problems state that the following points should be addressed (Department of Health, 1996):

- the person's past history
- the person's current state of mind, behaviour and outlook
- what the person reports at the time
- are there any discrepancies between what the person says and does?
- circumstances under which, based on past experience, this particular person has presented an increased risk
- have all risk factors been considered?
- does the risk assessment focus on evidence not just opinion?
- is it clear where the evidence has come from?
- have all relevant parties been consulted?

The last point on the list reinforces the need for good liaison and communication between different agencies that come into contact with people with mental health problems. A collaborative relationship between the police and mental health services may enable the police to gain information about a suspect if that person is already known to services.

When people with mental health problems are in custody it is also worth considering these additional points:

- tell the person what you are doing (they may appear not to understand or to listen but may in fact be listening and understanding)
- listen to the person and be seen to listen

- be calm, be seen to be calm and take your time (if possible)
- do not join in with someone if they appear to be deluded or hallucinating; it will confuse them and can appear patronising to pretend that you share their reality when you do not
- do make it clear that though you do not share their beliefs you accept that they feel the way they do, see the things they see or hear the things they do
- do not try to argue someone out of a delusion or a hallucination in a rational way; it is unlikely to be possible and may agitate the person or cause them to withdraw
- in particular do not argue with someone who appears to be paranoid, the person could become very threatened if their view of the world is being challenged and could become aggressive or even violent
- if someone seems to take a long time to answer give them the time, or perhaps rephrase your question or comment
- do not use language such as 'nutter', 'barking' which is offensive, insensitive and potentially oppressive

The nature, frequency and recognition of mental health problems

It is not easy to define what constitutes 'mental health' or 'having a mental health problem' and precise definitions for practical use are not available. Although 'mental illness' is the classification under which most patients are detained in hospital, it is not defined in the 1983 Mental Health Act. Someone is usually considered to be suffering from mental health problems if their mental distress appears out of proportion to, or does not fit, the circumstances in which they find themselves. Therefore, when deciding if someone has a mental health problem, behaviour, mood and perceptions are being judged in relation to what is considered normal, taking into account the individual's personal experiences and history, social world, culture, gender, race and age.

Mental health problems cover a wide range of conditions. It is usually thought of as a continuum from minor distress to severe disorder of mind or behaviour. It is a transitory rather than a permanent state and therefore whenever there is doubt about a suspect's mental state, a second opinion should always be sought, in order to assess the suspects' fitness for interview and/or detention.

The following is not an exhaustive list but are points worth bearing in mind when trying to decide if a suspect is suffering from a mental health problem and therefore has the right to the services of an Appropriate Adult.

- Does the person's behaviour fit with what would generally be expected of them considering their age, gender, ethnic origin, race, and cultural and social background?
- If the answer to any of the above is no, is there an explanation?
- Does the person react to you and to other people in a way that makes sense in terms of the situation?
- Does the person look strange given who they are and where they are?
- Is the person very difficult to engage and taking a long time to answer questions?
- Does the person not seem to know where they are or what they are doing?
- Does what the person say make sense, given who they are and where they are?
- Does it make sense some of the time and at other times not?

Research suggests that at any one time one in six adults suffers from one or other form of mental health problem (Bird, 1999). This makes mental health problems as common as asthma and it is estimated that 25 per cent of all routine GP consultation are people with mental health problems (Department of Health 1999). More women than men are diagnosed as having mental health problems: 20 per cent of women and 14 per cent of men (Bird, 1999). Severe mental health problems needing professional help is as common as heart disease and three times as common as cancer (Department of Health, 1999).

People of African-Caribbean origin are twice as likely as white people to be diagnosed with a mental health problem (Department of Health, 1999) whilst people from any Asian group appear to have a lower rate of mental health problems than white people (Nazroo, 1997). Interview surveys of large populations in the UK suggest that the key factor in explaining the different rates of mental health problems in different ethnic groups is socio-economic position rather than ethnicity itself. Research also suggests that assessments and diagnosis based on Western models of mental health problems are inappropriate for use among culturally different groups (Nazroo, 1997).

It is estimated that approximately 66 per cent of people on remand in England and Wales have a mental health problem (Bird, 1999). Nearly 14 per cent of the total prison population in England and Wales is considered to have a mental health problem and a prisoner is estimated to be seven times more likely to die from suicide than the general population (Bird, 1999).

Depression

Gudjonsson found that depression was the mental health problem least often identified by the police (Gudjonsson *et al.*, 1993).

What are the signs of depression?

In custody, people who are depressed may present some or all the following features: downcast eyes, difficulty in maintaining eye contact, reduced concentration and poor memory. People who are depressed will lack energy and their movement, speech and thinking will be slowed down compared to their usual way of functioning when not depressed. Depressed people feel exhausted and present as sad, hopeless or in a 'flat' mood. It is common for people who are depressed also to feel anxious, and decision making can be difficult. If someone is severely depressed they may take less care than normal with dress and personal hygiene.

In extreme situations the person may have delusions and hallucinations, usually associated with being bad, worthless and the cause of disaster, illness and so on. Low self-esteem, worthlessness and guilt are very common feelings in people who are depressed. It is not difficult to imagine that a very depressed person may either make false confessions or self-incriminating statements when faced with the stress of a police interview.

Not all the above signs will be present at all times in everyone who is depressed and the list should be considered a broad checklist.

How common is depression?

It is estimated that at any one time 10 per cent of the general population complain of some degree of depression and that 5 per cent will have a severe depression. About one in five adults suffer depression at some time in their lives (Department of Health, 1999).

Women are at least twice as likely as men to be diagnosed as depressed: each year one woman in fifteen and one man in thirty will be affected by depression (Bird, 1999).

Asian women are more likely than white women to be diagnosed depressed and the suicide rate for South Asian women is particularly high. African-Caribbean women are less likely than white women to be diagnosed depressed (Bird, 1999).

Interview surveys suggest that people of African-Caribbean origin have a higher rate of depression than white people. However, they are less likely to have their depression recognised and to receive a service than are white people (Nazroo, 1997).

Risk of crime and suicide

People who are depressed have a lower risk of crime than the general population and there is no connection between depression and crimes involving violence. There is a possible connection between depression and shoplifting, particularly in middle aged and elderly people. The act may not be because of criminal intent but rather the result of absent-mindedness. People who are experiencing delusions may commit offences as they act upon the delusion and a suicide attempt may cause harm to property or other people (Department of Health, 1994).

People who are depressed are far more likely to harm themselves than others. Approximately 15 per cent of people who are depressed will eventually kill themselves. Seventy percent of suicides are by people who have experienced some form of depression (Bird 1999).

Manic Depression

People with manic depression have recurrent episodes of severe depression and of abnormally elevated mood, known as mania. In between episodes of being very low or very high people usually have periods when they are well.

For the main signs of depression, and risks associated with depression see the section above.

What are the signs of mania?

The signs of mania are the opposite of the signs of depression. People who are manic may present in police custody with some or all of the following features: hyperactivity, excited mood, rapid and possibly loud speech which is often difficult to follow. The person will experience a markedly increased level of energy compared to their usual way of functioning. They may be unable to sit still or to settle and will have grandiose thoughts about themselves, ranging from inflated self-opinion to delusions about their own abilities. Someone who is manic will appear to lack awareness of the impact of their behaviour which can be very extravagant, such as spending vast amounts of money or planning a scheme to save the world. Someone who is manic is likely to be very irritated or angry if people try to stop them carrying out their plans.

Not all the above signs will be present at all times in everyone who has manic depression and the list should be considered a broad checklist.

How common is manic depression?

It is estimated that one in a hundred adults in the UK will experience manic depression at some point in their life (Bird, 1999). The rate is similar for men and for women.

Risk of crime and suicide:
Public order offences are more likely than in the general population because of loud, exaggerated behaviour. The manic person may harm themselves or other people because they are unaware of dangers at the time (University of Manchester and Department of Health, 1996).

There is an increased risk of violence if the person is prevented from doing something that to them seems rational and obvious.

People who are manic are very unlikely to kill themselves deliberately. They may die accidentally because they disregard risks to their own safety (University of Manchester and Department of Health, 1996).

Schizophrenia
As mentioned above, research suggests that the police are most likely to identify mental disorder in suspects who are behaving in a bizarre way and exhibiting florid psychotic symptoms (Evans and Rawstorne, 1997). Gudjonsson *et al.*, (1993) found that suspects with schizophrenia are the group of people with mental health problems most readily identified by the police (Gudjonsson *et al.*, 1993).

What are the signs of schizophrenia?
The diagnosis of schizophrenia covers a range of conditions. People who are diagnosed with schizophrenia usually have long periods where they do not suffer from active symptoms and the features described below are present when someone is in a florid state.

1.   Audio or visual hallucinations: the person is hearing one or more voices which are not heard by anyone else or seeing things not seen by other people present.

2.   Delusion: a fixed belief that is not consistent with the cultural and intellectual beliefs in the society or culture in which the person is living. With a persecutory delusion the person feels under threat or attack.

3.   Thought disorder: sufferers may experience thoughts that are not their own; a sense that thoughts are being removed from their mind; or feel that their thoughts can be shared with other people without any speech. There may also be a disturbance of the process of thinking and an

inability to focus on the main point of a statement or an argument. If someone appears distracted or perplexed this may be because they are preoccupied with delusions or hallucinations. If people are thought – disordered or are having delusions or hallucinations at the time of the interview they are likely to have impaired or distorted memory both of the interview and of the events about which they are being questioned.

4. Mood disorder: this may be incongruity of mood where the mood does not fit the context – for instance laughter when sadness seems more appropriate – or 'blunting' of mood where the person appears to lack the ability to express deep emotion (also often called lacking in affect). Apparent abnormalities of mood, movements and speech may be less abnormal in the context of the individual's delusion, hallucination or thought disorder. Frequently, however, no one else is aware of the exact nature of the thought disorder, delusions and hallucinations.

Not all the above signs will be present at all times in everyone who has been diagnosed with schizophrenia and the list should be considered a broad checklist.

How common is schizophrenia?
It is estimated that 1 per cent of the adult population will suffer from schizophrenia at some time. Approximately 25 per cent will make a good recovery after one schizophrenic episode; two-thirds will have repeated episodes with florid symptoms and some degree of disability in relation to social functioning; and approximately 10–15 per cent will develop severe long-term disabilities in relation to daily living skills and social functioning (University of Manchester and Department of Health, 1996; Department of Health, 1999).

The peak age for diagnosing schizophrenia is between 35 and 39. Men are more likely than women to be diagnosed as having schizophrenia before the age of 45 but after this age more women than men are diagnosed as having schizophrenia (Bird, 1999).

Research suggests that African-Caribbean men and women are 3–5 times more likely than white people to be diagnosed and admitted to hospital with schizophrenia. African-Caribbean people diagnosed with schizophrenia are $2\frac{1}{2}$ times more likely than white people to have poor outcome from treatment (Bird, 1999). Interview surveys suggest that African-Caribbean people may have the same rate of schizophrenia as white people. The apparent higher rate may be due to mental health services' failure to engage appropriately with people of

African-Caribbean origin (Nazroo, 1997). Studies of mental health problems in people of Asian origin are inconclusive. The rate of schizophrenia appears to be similar to white people but the recovery rate appears to be better (Nazroo, 1997).

Research suggests that between 30 per cent and 50 per cent of homeless people have a severe mental health problem, mainly schizophrenia (Bird, 1999). Misuse of alcohol and drugs is high in people diagnosed with schizophrenia, and figures vary from 20 per cent to 50 per cent (Bird, 1999).

Risk of crime and suicide
The data from studies comparing the rate of violence by people treated for schizophrenia and by the general population vary considerably. In general the majority of studies find that people with schizophrenia commit more violent acts than the general population in terms of self-reported violence, arrests and convictions for violence. The figures vary between men and women: men with schizophrenia are four times more violent than men in the general population whilst the difference between women in the two groups is much higher (Jewesbury *et al.*, 1998).

A large population survey on self reported violence in USA found that 8 per cent of people with schizophrenia reported they had been violent in the last 12 months. This figure was four times greater than in people without mental health problems, even when account was taken of gender, age and socio-economic status (Swanson *et al.*, 1990).

As discussed in the section above on 'Crime and People with Mental Health Problems' the proportion of homicides committed by people with mental health problems has declined from 50 per cent to 14 per cent since the 1960s. It is estimated that 0.4 per cent of the population in England and Wales has schizophrenia, yet they account for between 4 per cent and 6 per cent of all homicides (Jewesbury *et al.*, 1998). The link between risk of homicide and schizophrenia is complex. However, there seems little doubt that a diagnosis of schizophrenia is associated with an increased risk of violence and even homicide.

It is important to distinguish between the risk when a person with a diagnosis of schizophrenia is florid – is actively psychotic – and the risk when the person is in a more stable frame of mind. The risk of violence is increased if someone with schizophrenia is experiencing persecutory delusions or 'command' hallucinations (that is, hearing voices telling them to kill particular people). Generally delusions are more common triggers for violence than hallucinations.

People with schizophrenia may commit crimes such as public order offences when they are deluded or have hallucinations. They may also have difficulties maintaining a stable life style and therefore be at greater risk of committing minor offences associated with obtaining food and shelter (University of Manchester and DoH, 1996). Bizarre violence to self is strongly associated with schizophrenia, such as self-mutilation (University of Manchester and DoH, 1999). People who misuse drugs or alcohol are twice as likely to be violent as people diagnosed with schizophrenia (Ward and Applin, 1998).

People with schizophrenia are significantly more likely to commit suicide than the general population: between 9 per cent and 13 per cent of people with schizophrenia are likely to commit suicide (Bird, 1999).

See also the section on 'Crime and People with Mental Health Problems' above.

Anxiety states

Gudjonsson *et.al.* found that 20 per cent of suspects in custody were suffering from an abnormally high level of anxiety (Gudjonsson *et.al.*, 1993). This figure is considerably higher than the estimate for anxiety states in the adult population in general. The stress of being a suspect would be a contributory factor to this. A large proportion of people with other psychiatric diagnoses also suffer from anxiety states. The stress and subsequently heightened state of anxiety is a crucial issue when deciding if someone with a history of mental health problems needs the services of an Appropriate Adult.

What are the signs of anxiety states?
In general people will be considered to be suffering from an anxiety state if the level, frequency and length of the anxiety make it difficult for them to carry on with a normal life. The person may have somatic symptoms such as headaches, stomach aches and muscle tension; their mood may change frequently, and appetite and sleep may be disturbed (they may sleep or eat more or less than is usual for them). The anxiety may manifest itself through phobic disorders, such as fear of open places, enclosed spaces, spiders, dirt and so on. Another manifestation is obsessional disorders where the person's thoughts and behaviour is centred on a particular person or problem in a manner which is out of proportion to the situation. People with anxiety states may have panic attacks where they get overwhelmed by severe and crippling anxiety.

Not all the above signs of anxiety states will be present at all times in everyone who suffers an abnormally high level of anxiety. The list should be used as a general guideline only.

How common are anxiety states?

It is estimated that more than one in ten people are likely to have a disabling anxiety at some point and that up to 13 per cent of the adult population will develop a phobia at some stage. This may have little influence on their ability to carry on with their life, or may be severely disabling (Bird, 1999). Anxiety accounts for one in ten of all new episodes of diagnosed mental health problems and it is estimated that one third of all mental health problems seen by GPs are due to anxiety (Department of Health, 1999).

People with high levels of anxiety frequently have a higher than average rate of substance abuse (Department of Health, 1999).

Risk of crime and suicide:

People with anxiety states are no more likely to commit crimes than the general population. They are mainly focused on their own feelings and anxieties and are much more likely to harm themselves than other people (Department of Health, 1994).

No separate figures relating suicide and anxiety states are available. Anxiety is very common in people with depression (see section on 'Depression' above).

Personality disorders

Personality disorder is a broad category and the definitions tend to vary between cultures and countries. The disorder is considered to be an intrinsic part of someone's personality. If someone has previously been behaving normally and then changes their behaviour the explanation may be that they are ill. People who have always behaved differently and whose behaviour 'just gets worse' are often said to have a personality disorder. The term tends to be used to describe persistently odd, anti-social or dangerous behaviour. Personality disorders cover a range of different groups of behaviour patterns and the personality disorder can be of different types (for example, psycho-pathic, antisocial, histrionic and inadequate). The definition of the various subcategories of personality disorders has varied over time and the psycho-pathic or antisocial personal disorders are most closely linked to risk of crime, including the risk of violence. The vast majority of people diagnosed with personality disorders present no higher risk of crime than the general population. However, the small group of people with psychopathic personal-ity disorders causes a considerable concern and challenge to both mental health services and to the criminal justice system.

There is considerable controversy about whether personality disorder should be a psychiatric term and whether people with personality disorder can or should be treated within mental health services. It is very difficult to change – and to treat – someone with a personality disorder, and people with this diagnosis are often excluded from the mental health service. It is now generally acknowledged that the current legal framework in this country does not provide either help for people with personality disorders or safeguards for the protection of the public. The Government recently published new proposals for changes to both services and legislation (Home Office and Department of Health, 1999).

What are the signs of personality disorder?
The list would be very long and is beyond the scope of this chapter. However, the common feature is behaviour which significantly deviates from what is regarded morally acceptable, thereby causing difficulties in social functioning. The behaviour and attitudes tend to be very difficult to change and will often have started in late childhood, developed during adolescence and will continue into adulthood.

How common are personality disorders?
About 10–15 per cent of the population is considered to have a personality disorder. The figures vary in relation to the various subcategories of personality disorders.

Risks of crime and suicide
The definition of personality disorder includes 'unacceptable behaviour or attitudes' and, in the case of psychopathic personality disorder, also a disposition to behave violently. It is therefore to be expected that people with personality disorders have a higher risk of committing crimes than the general population.

It is estimated that up to 70 per cent of the prison population has a personality disorder (Department of Health, 1994). These figures cover a wide variety of crimes: crimes against property and against other people are associated with some categories of personality disorder. Some crimes against the person may well involve the threat or use of violence.

It is estimated that 15 per cent of people with personality disorder will eventually die from suicide (Department of Health, 1994).

Conclusion
Suspects with mental health problems have a right to the services of an Appropriate Adult and it is crucial that the police have the skills and confidence to identify and deal sympathetically and effectively with people in

custody who may have mental health problems in custody. Definition of mental health and identification of people with mental health problems is not straightforward, and the link between mental health problems and risk of crime is complex. The identification of mental health problems needs to be based on an individual assessment of each individual person, and not solely on broad diagnostic categories.

Research suggests that the police need further training in mental health in order to ensure that people who are entitled to an Appropriate Adult are given this service. Improved liaison with specialist mental health services would enable the police to check if someone has mental health problems if they are already 'known'. Closer links with other agencies could also be a rich source for inter-professional and inter-agency training and professional development, enabling the police to develop their skills and knowledge in relation to people with mental health problems as well as giving other professionals the opportunity to understand the role of an Appropriate Adult and the role of the police in this process.

Given the problems outlined in this and other chapters in this book, there appears to be a strong case for the development and improvement of Appropriate Adult schemes so that the difficulties of gaining the attendance of properly trained and supported Appropriate Adults do not influence the judgement of vulnerability, thereby depriving people with mental health problems of this service.

References :

Appleby, I, Shaw, J, Amos, T and McDonnell, R (1999) *Safer Services. National confidential inquiry into suicides and homicides by people with mental illness*. London, Department of Health.

Bird, L (1999) *The Fundamental Facts. All the latest facts and figures on mental illness* London, The Mental Health Foundation.

Department of Health (1994) *Working with Mentally Disordered Offenders, A training pack for social services staff and others dealing with mentally disordered offenders* London, NACRO.

Department of Health (1996) *Building Bridges. A guide to arrangements for interagency working for the care and protection of mentally ill people* London, HMSO.

Department of Health (1999) *National Service Framework for Mental Health. Modern Standards and Service Models* London, Stationery Office.

Evans, R and Rawstorne, S (1997) 'Appropriate Behaviour'. *Community Care* 17–23 July pp. 30-31.

Gudjonsson, G, Clare, I and Rutter, S (1993) 'Persons at risk during interviews in police custody: the identification of vulnerabilities, Research Study No.12' *The Royal Commission on Criminal Justice* London, HMSO.

Home Office (1995a) *Appropriate Adults: Report of Review Group* London, Home Office.

Home Office (1995b) *Police and Criminal Evidence Act. 1984 Code of Practice B–E*, London, HMSO.

Home Office and Department of Health (1999) *Managing Dangerous People with Severe Personality Disorder. Proposal for Policy Development*, London. HMSO.

Jewesbury, J, Sandell, G. and Allen, R. (eds.) (1998) *Risks and Rights: Mentally Disturbed Offenders and Public Protection* London, NACRO.

Nazroo, J Y (1997) *Ethnicity and Mental Health: fourth national survey of ethnic minorities* London, Policy Studies Institute.

Pearse, J (1995) 'Police Interviewing: The Identification of Vulnerabilities'. *Journal of Community & Applied Psychology* .5, pp.1147–59.

Reith, M (1998) *Community Care Tragedies: A practical guide to mental health inquiries* London, Venture Press.

Stanley, N, Manthorpe, J and Penhale, B (eds.) (1999) *Institutional Abuse: perspectives across the life course* London, Routledge.

Swanson, J, Holzer, C, Ganju, V and Tsutomo Jono, R 'Violence and Psychiatric Disorder in the Community. Evidence from the Epidemiological Catchment Area Studies' *Hospital and Community Psychiatry* 41, pp 761–70

Taylor, P J and Gunn, J (1999) 'Homicides by People with Mental Illness: Myth or Reality' *British Journal of Psychiatry* p. 174.

University of Manchester and Department of Health (1996) *Risk Assessment: Learning materials on mental health* Manchester, University of Manchester.

Ward, M and Applin, C (1998) *The Unlearned Lesson: The role of alcohol and drug misuse in homicides perpetrated by people with mental health problems* London, Wynne Howard.

Chapter 6
Learning Disabilities: One person's use

Debra Fearns

The Police and Criminal Evidence Act (PACE) 1984, and its accompanying Codes of Practice were introduced following the report of the Royal Commission on Criminal Procedure (Philips, 1981). The PACE Codes of Practice (Home Office1995) set out guidelines regarding the detention and questioning of those suspects who might have a mental disorder, including learning disabilities.

Code C, paragraph 11b, makes it very clear that potentially vulnerable suspects need further protection, and states that:

It is important to bear in mind that, although juveniles or persons who are mentally ill or mentally handicapped are often capable of providing reliable evidence, they may without knowing or wishing to do so, be particularly prone in certain circumstances to provide knowledge and information that is unreliable, misleading or self-incriminating.

This chapter seeks to explore the experience of one individual with a learning disability, and to examine further the difficulties faced by individuals who have a learning disability. The interview is supplemented with commentary and relevant extra information. Additionally, the process of identifying 'vulnerable' suspects from the custody officers' perspective will be examined from research carried out with custody officers in a Shire police force, and guidelines on recognition of suspects with a learning disability presented.

One learning disabled person's experiences of detention
Ian (a pseudonym) is a well-built man in his early forties. He has a beard and black hair. When I met him, it was winter, and he was dressed in black, with black gloves and a black woolly hat. On first impressions, he looked an imposing figure.

He has lived in a busy town for a number of years, and has a support worker from Social Services who remains in regular contact with him. He lives alone, and presents as a solitary person with an abiding interest in photography.

The purpose of the interview with Ian was to find out how he experienced the role of the Appropriate Adult and his treatment by the police.

DF: How did the police officers treat you at the Police Station?

Ian: Some are OK, some not ... depends on attitude. Some are big-headed.

DF: Are most big-headed?

Ian: Hard to say ... about half and half.

DF: Why were you in the police station?

Ian: Someone lied to the police and said I've taken pictures I shouldn't have. That I'd asked children to take their clothes off.

DF: Do you know who it was?

Ian: Someone who knows me, you could say. I don't know who it is, but they don't like me, and the police don't understand. I suffer with epilepsy – but someone threw stones at me, and I went off my head , and hit them. [This was not the reason he was held at the Police Station].

DF: What did the police officers in the station say to you?

Ian: A policeman said: 'Do you know why you're here?' I said: 'Yes, I haven't done anything wrong.' The policeman said: 'Can you read words?' When I shook my head, he then added: 'You need glasses then.' I said: 'I don't, my eyesight's fine.'

When asked why he thought the policeman had said that to him, Ian's response was 'they try to get their own back'. He said he thought they didn't like him, that's why they were not nice to him.

DF: Did they ask you if you wanted an Appropriate Adult to be involved in your interview?

Ian: The policeman called the Appropriate Adult. He wasn't very nice, either. I was scratching myself, and the Appropriate Adult said: 'You've got fleas.' I said: 'How do you know I've got fleas?' but he didn't answer.

DF: Did you know who the Appropriate Adult was going to be, or were you asked to name a person already known to you?

Ian: No, the Appropriate Adult was already in the Police Station. I didn't know him. He wasn't helpful. I told him I couldn't hurt children.

DF: Did the policeman explain why you were in the police station?

Ian: I didn't really understand. The policeman and Appropriate Adult asked me if I could read. I said 'No' and was insulted by both of them. The Appropriate Adult didn't know what he was doing, and he annoyed me.

DF: Were you told why the Appropriate Adult was there?

Ian: No.

DF: Were you given a choice of Appropriate Adult?

Ian: No, no one told me anything. I had heard somewhere, though, that the Appropriate Adult should be there with the solicitor.

DF: Was the Appropriate Adult helpful?

Ian: No, he wasn't helpful. I told him I couldn't hurt children. He didn't know what he was doing. If an Appropriate Adult is to be there when a person is being questioned, they should be more understanding. I told the policeman who my solicitor was. They rang my doctor, 'cos they thought I was carrying drugs. [Ian had his medication for his epilepsy with him].
When my solicitor came, he said two words, I got up and that was it.

Ian was clearly unhappy with his experience. His support worker was present during this interview with the author, and with Ian's permission, added additional information where she thought it would be helpful. The support worker said that Ian had psoriasis, hence the scratching observed by the Appropriate Adult. She explained that Ian's psoriasis often became worse when he was stressed and that Ian is embarrassed by his need to scratch. The support worker also said that Ian's main focus in life is his hobby of photography. Ian showed me some of his collection of photographs that consist mainly of images of animals, some of people. They are inoffensive, amateur snaps taken on an ordinary Instamatic camera. However, Ian always has his camera, and is often taking photographs, but not always with the consent or agreement of the people 'snapped'.

He is a well-known figure in the town, but his habit of catching people on film has caused him to be banned from one of the main shopping centres whilst he is in possession of his camera.

During the interview, Ian told of another occasion of being questioned by the police whilst he was waiting outside the local spiritualist church. He was standing outside the church early one morning. He was two hours early, as the church did not open until 11 a.m. Ian apparently prefers to be early for things, rather than late, so it is not unusual for him to appear to be 'hanging around' without purpose. He said two plainclothes policemen came up to him and asked him what he was doing. At the time, he was wearing his black, woolly hat, black gloves, black jeans and a black bomber jacket. When Ian explained his reasons for being there, the two policemen said sorry to him and left him alone.

Ian said he thought that, generally, people are too suspicious.

Ian was asked what advice he would give to the police to help people with learning disabilities in these situations.

If a person hasn't got a solicitor, they should find someone who has more love and understanding – if they're worse than I am, they need someone. The police need to have more love and understanding and not be against the person.

The Custody Officer needs to listen to people better, and some are ignorant and need to look at attitudes. Asking me to read when it's late and too hard.

Ian's experience is negative with regard both to the policemen he came into contact with, and to the Appropriate Adult. His support worker said that the police did not inform them that Ian had been in police custody, and that they had not been asked to provide an Appropriate Adult. She also commented that it was highly irregular for an Appropriate Adult to be introduced to a suspect without prior knowledge or information, and for the Appropriate Adult to be someone who was there just because he had been involved in another case.

Overall, Ian has a very poor view of the police, and was scathing of the usefulness of his Appropriate Adult. He felt that the Appropriate Adult was on the side of the police, not there to support him. The Appropriate Adult was also rude and offensive, which meant that he was not ideally placed to ensure that Ian was comfortable and at ease, and that he understood what he was being questioned about.

Custody officers: recognition and treatment of people with learning disabilities
In 1998, I carried out a series of interviews with custody officers' in a Shire county as part of my research for a Master's Degree, leading to the presentation of an unpublished dissertation (Fearns,1998a). These findings were

presented at a British Association of Social Workers' Conference in October 1997, and published as conference proceedings, entitled 'Appropriate Adults and Vulnerable Groups in Custody, A Collection of papers from a One Day Conference.' (Fearns, 1998b).

Initially fifty postal questionnaires were sent to custody areas throughout the county. The return rate was 42 per cent. The questionnaire was designed to be open-ended, and the purpose was to ascertain the ways in which custody officers identified 'vulnerability.'

The questionnaires comprised twelve questions requiring an explanation or understanding of custody officers' own perceptions and understanding of 'vulnerability' in relation to the PACE Codes of Practice. The theme of the first three questions was identification of 'vulnerability' within potential suspects, coupled with their own view of their competence and confidence to carry out that task.

The theme of questions 4–7 was differentiation of learning disability and mental illness, and the third theme, covering questions 8–10, was of the use and usefulness of 'appropriate adults', within a six-month time span. The fourth and final theme was to ascertain their thoughts and/or views on ways of improving the identification of vulnerable suspects. A final section encouraged custody officers to add any other information or comments that they felt were relevant to this subject area.

All the returned questionnaires gave comprehensive answers to the first seven questions, indicating that custody officers (COs) had a keen interest in, and possible concerns about, the identification of vulnerability.

With regard to question 1, it is not difficult to categorise the responses to 'List and describe the signs or signals which might lead you to think that a suspect may be "vulnerable"'; and a number of similar words recurred, including:

'Unusual behaviour' (CO7)

'Erratic mood changes' (CO10)

'Appears vague and is confused' (CO12)

'Demeanour' (CO19)

A significant number of responses indicated that custody officers seemed to use four main types of criterion for describing the signs or signals relating to vulnerability. These are broadly:

- appearance and/or demeanour
- ability to read and write
- ability to understand what is being said to them
- erratic or unusual behaviour

These responses indicate that there is a need for explicit and clearly defined guidelines to be available in custody suites to enable custody officers to carry out their role more effectively. Evidently the criteria used by custody officers can lead to vulnerability being missed - see also Chapter 3 by John Pearse. Whilst appearance and demeanour can aid detection, in themselves they are not reliable indicators. Used in combination with assessing erratic or unusual behaviour, they may have more value in helping to detect signs of mental illness. However, these two criteria are heavily subjective, and what one custody officer may see as a sign of vulnerability, another may choose to ignore.

Using literacy levels also has its dangers. It is true that extra care may need to be taken in ensuring that suspects are helped to understand what they are being held for, and may need clarification of their rights. However, it is not inevitable that such a person will require the assistance of an Appropriate Adult as illiteracy does not necessarily indicate intellectual impairment.

The criterion that is probably most effective in indicating vulnerability is number 3; the ability to understand what is being said to them. If any of the other three criteria are also present, it could be reasonably said that this suspect is vulnerable. If a suspect is obviously unable to make sense of why he or she is being held in custody, clearly there is a need for the custody officer to take note and introduce either an Appropriate Adult or the Forensic Medical Examiner, or both.

The data suggest that not all custody officers use all four criteria, so if a custody officer only relies on criterion 1 or 4, for example, vulnerability may well remain unidentified.

There should be concerns about a number of the custody officers who returned questionnaires, as they described signs that are normally associated with physical illness. For example, CO17 listed: 'drunkenness, drugs, social status, incoherent speech', while CO11 described: 'dishevelled appearance, tics and twitches, incoherent speech, and strange phrases'.

These responses suggest that there is a confusion about suspects who may be vulnerable, and bears out the findings of Bean and Nemitz (1994), and

Palmer and Hart (1996), that custody officers are competent in identifying certain forms of mental illness, but are much less successful in identifying people with learning disabilities.

The custody officers were confident they could make appropriate judgements about a suspect's vulnerability. Only a few officers felt that they were 'quite confident'. Replies included

Very confident – assessments I have made have been confirmed by police doctor at a later stage. (CO16).

Extremely confident; custody officer for over five years and dealt with thousands of prisoners (CO10)

Very confident, I have had experience of dealing with all types of vulnerable persons (CO13)

Confident about making a judgement, experience being the main reason If in any doubt, call the Forensic Medical Examiner (CO12).

There may be two reasons for custody officers stating that they are confident when making a judgement about vulnerability. First, one could expect them to be confident as it is a key part of the custody officers' job. It would be difficult to admit to doubts regarding an inability to carry out this role effectively. Second, judgements can only be made against prior knowledge and experience. Therefore, they rightly feel that they are confident and competent, as prior experience has not actively challenged their perceptions in a formal way. As one reply stated 'I know how to spot someone who is "not quite all there"' (CO19).

Other questions asked whether there are differences between a person with a learning disability and a person with a mental illness. The responses indicate that there is a degree of confusion about the nature of learning disability. This confirms that there are real problems when it comes to identifying vulnerable suspects who have a learning disability. This is highlighted in research by Gudjonsson *et al* (1993).

Differentiating between learning disability, literacy difficulties, and mental health problems

The research findings indicate that there are two particular areas to be addressed in relation to recognition. These concern the differentiation between learning disabilities and mental health problems, and the confusion related to literacy.

All the custody officers agreed that there was a difference between learning disability and mental illness, yet when further asked to describe these differences, three custody officers were unable to be specific about what these could be. The reasons given were:

Too many to list in this space. (CO16).

There is a difference in law as regards an AA [Appropriate Adult] (CO17).

Too complex to consider here (CO21).

These three custody officers had previously indicated on the questionnaire that they were confident of recognising vulnerability, but their responses illustrate that there are problems. The remaining custody officers tried to describe the differences between a person with a learning disability and a person with a mental illness, but they were not always successful. Custody officer 2, for example, wrote:

The person with a learning disability may be just unable to read or write properly or be unable to understand simple instructions/procedures, whereas the mentally disordered offender may be suffering from delusions, fantasies and so on.

Given the level of confusion and misconception within society as a whole regarding the differences between people with a learning disability and those with mental health needs, this is clearly an area that warrants further study.

Following on from the postal questionnaires, ten custody officers were interviewed face-to-face. Each interview took between 45 minutes and one hour. The custody officers were unknown to me but selection was purposive, in the sense that I wished to interview at least one officer from each of the nine designated custody suites in operation across the county. This would provide data that could offer comparisons across the county, if necessary.

What some of the answers revealed was the earlier problem of differentiating illiteracy from intellectual impairment. Custody officer 5 stated that: 'learning disability would have a more definite pattern of behaviour. Learning difficulty is for life.' Custody officer 6 seemed to have a misunderstanding that could have an impact on whether a suspect with a learning disability would receive the services of an Appropriate Adult. He stated: 'A person with a learning disability would not require the assistance of an expert, whereas a mental illness could be restrictive and prevent an interview from taking place.'

The use of appropriate adults

A series of questions was asked concerning the role of the Appropriate Adult. However, this information is not generalisable, although it could have been if a pilot survey had been carried out. It would have then been possible to distinguish between the use of Appropriate Adults for juveniles, and people with a mental disorder, or learning disabilities. None the less, 8 of the custody officers themselves identified that most often the Appropriate Adult was used for juveniles. However, a broad analysis can be suggested. Four custody officers during the six-month time-span did not use an Appropriate Adult, and the average frequency was 7. In line with previous findings (Gudjonsson *et al.*, 1993; Bean and Nemitz 1994; Palmer and Hart, 1996), it could be argued that custody officers are failing to protect the interests of vulnerable suspects.

Custody officer 15 identified that although he had used an Appropriate Adult on up to 60 occasions, it was mostly for juveniles. (See Chapter 3 by John Pearse).

The final questions asked the custody officers to make comments about how identification could be improved. Around 80 per cent of the responses indicated that training was needed, and not just for the police, but also for Forensic Medical Examiners and some said for Approved Social Workers. Custody officer 3 summed up the feelings of the majority of respondents as 'Some training, anything, would be better than nothing, which is the current situation.'

A number of other custody officers also remarked that it would be useful to be able to identify 'known' vulnerable suspects through the Police National Computer (PNC). It has to be said, though, that this method may not only be fallible but also raises ethical issues that would be of concern.

The interviews shed light on some of the written replies, but did not substantially affect the analysis and conclusions that were drawn from these replies. Custody officer 9, when asked how confident he was in making a judgement regarding vulnerability, said: 'I have no qualifications and have to rely on my own observations and judgements — but I'm fairly confident.' This was echoed by custody officer 4 who stated that: 'Skills are picked up through experience, or what might be known as "muddling through".' Those custody officers interviewed also reiterated that they relied almost exclusively on intuition and experience in detecting vulnerability.

This reliance on experience exposes the weaknesses of using the custody officer in the role of 'gate-keeper' in the implementation of PACE. It verifies that a lack of appropriate training in learning disabilities and mental health has an impact on the effectiveness of custody officers' ability to carry out their role. Custody officer 7 noted that the training to be a custody officer is very thorough, but it is weighted towards procedural and legal issues, and does not cover the recognition of vulnerable suspects. These interviews amplified the response of the questionnaires, and were useful in enabling custody officers to talk about their role. At the same time, it gave them the opportunity to expand on areas of concern from their perspective, and provided additional material worthy of further research.

The available evidence demonstrates that when it comes to identifying vulnerable suspects in need of an Appropriate Adult, the police, in general, are failing. This is due to a number of factors that the data confirm.

Identifying and understanding the levels of learning disability
Often, the term learning disability is qualified by 'mild', 'moderate' or 'profound'. These adjectives are usually based on a combination of the severity of the individual's disability and their IQ measures. The most difficult group to identify are those people with a mild learning disability, in the IQ range of 55–69. The IQ of the average person is 100. The difficulties faced by this group of people are multi-faceted, and arise because of public and professional prejudices and misunderstandings.

Self-identification
For a person with a learning disability, everyday life can pose a number of challenges. One of these challenges is to process and make sense of words and their meanings in order to understand what other people might require from them. To have to ask for help can be a burden for many of us, yet for a person with a learning disability it can lead to embarrassment, ridicule and humiliation. Additionally, having to seek assistance and actively identify 'special' needs can have a devastating effect on a person with a learning disability leading to differential treatment (as experienced by Ian).

It is therefore not surprising that research, such as Pearse (1995), and Lyall *et al.* (1995), has identified the difficulties faced by people with learning disabilities brought into the criminal justice system. This is partly due to the reluctance of people with learning disabilities to admit their difficulties and ask for help. The life experiences of this group of people have not always been positive; therefore many individuals have subsequently learned to 'hide' their disability. At the same time, their level of social functioning compensates for their difficulties of comprehension and understanding, and they therefore appear to be fully cognisant of what is happening to them, and give an impression of coping that belies the situation.

Some professionals may not perceive this to be their problem, and to an extent that point may have some validity. However, as professionals, certain duties are explicit within these roles, whilst other duties of providing appropriate care and protection are implicit. In particular, the police, solicitors, Forensic Medical Examiners and the Crown Prosecution Service need urgently to enhance their knowledge and understanding of people who have learning disabilities. Intellectual impairment is not by itself, an indicator that individuals are not capable of being helped to understand and participate in the judicial process.

Differentiation of learning disability and literacy skills
A real difficulty arises because a small, yet significant, number of custody officers was either unaware or unable to distinguish between an inability to read or write, and an inability to comprehend and recall information in a logical, reasoned manner. If, as might be the case, assumptions are made on the basis of literacy, clearly a number of suspects in need of protection as defined by the Codes of Practice will slip through the net. Assuming that illiteracy indicates a learning disability is equally erroneous, and has the potential to create a number of difficulties for both the police and the suspect.

Limited understanding of learning disabilities
This is a very real problem, not only for custody officers and other ranks of the police force, but also for some Appropriate Adults and Forensic Medical Examiners. Of course the problem is not theirs alone it is a much wider problem in society as a whole. There is a worrying level of ignorance, first about the difference between learning disabilities and mental health and, second, an understanding of what having an intellectual impairment means. Many people think it only applies to people who have a recognised syndrome, such as Down's Syndrome. It is not surprising that people's judgements are based on stereotypes and perceptions that have little basis in reality. The Codes of Practice can only be effective if custody officers are skilled enough to recognise the vulnerable suspect with a learning disability.

These factors are of equal relevance for people with mental health needs, although my own research, as well as research by Bean and Nemitz (1994), and Palmer and Hart (1996), suggests that custody officers are more able to identify suspects' vulnerability due to mental health needs. It is noted, too, that when suspects are in an acute stage of a mental illness, they usually exhibit florid signs that are difficult to miss. Mentally ill suspects are also more likely to tell the custody officer if they are receiving treatment. They also seem to be less inhibited in naming a contact person to support them.

The officers who participated in this research stated that they received much additional information on mental illness from their contact with Forensic Medical Examiners. In the interviews, the custody officers were asked to comment on their usefulness in aiding identification of vulnerability. Comments on their usefulness varied, depending on each area of the county. Custody officer 7 said: 'They are generally good. Those with lack of experience are not so good as they tend not to want to commit themselves – sometimes you have to press them for an opinion/judgement.'

Custody officer 1 said that he questioned the value of Forensic Medical Examiners, as 'most are local General Practitioners who may themselves not be experienced. We are caught in the middle of a contradiction. For example, 'time' versus 'fitness for detention.'

Again, officers could be helped to improve their knowledge of learning disability and mental illness through training and education.. They should also receive training to improve their understanding of physical illnesses that could be confused with mental illness, such as Transient Ischemic Attacks (commonly known as strokes) and hyperglycaemia.

Evidently, the focus for future research is centred on methods of identification. This applies not only to custody officers, but also to all ranks within the police force, Forensic Medical Examiners, social workers (including Approved Social Workers) and all other personnel involved in the criminal justice system.

The PACE Act Codes of Practice also make it explicit that if there is any doubt in the view of the custody officer as to whether a suspect may be deemed to be vulnerable, whether because they are juveniles, or because it is thought they may be 'mentally disordered' or 'mentally handicapped', an Appropriate Adult should attend any subsequent interviews to protect the vulnerable person. Yet the failing of these Codes has been readily identified: see, for example, Gudjonsson *et al.* (1993), Bean and Nemitz (1994) and Palmer and Hart (1996). Primarily, the failings can be accounted for in two main ways.

1. Codes of Practice, without the status of law, not only lack rigour, but are also not enforceable in the same way. Breaches are subject only to possible disciplinary procedures, or evidence being dismissed as a result of the Codes being broken.

2. The government has not resourced the Act, and have left police forces, social services departments and voluntary organisations to find their own ways of training and providing people to be appropriate adults.

The current provision is in need of reform, as there is clear evidence that custody officers are not as competent at recognising vulnerability as they believe they are. Additionally, Appropriate Adults are often ill informed as to the purpose of their role and are therefore largely ineffective at protecting the vulnerable suspect. The criminal justice system as a whole also needs to review the manner in which cases are reported, recorded – acted upon when the individual has a learning disability or mental health problem.

References

Bean, P and Nemitz, T (1994) *Out of depth and out of sight* London, Mencap.

Fearns, D (1998a) *'Analysis of the policy background relating to the PACE 1984 and its Codes of Practice and the methods used by custody officers in determining a suspect's vulnerability especially on relation to people with learning disabilities'*, Unpublished dissertation, London, University of Middlesex

Fearns, D (1998b) *Appropriate Adults and Vulnerable Groups in Custody, A collection of papers from a one day conference* Birmingham, British Association of Social Workers.

Gudjonsson, G, Clare, I and Rutter, S (1993) 'Persons at risk during interviews in police custody: the identification of vulnerabilities.' Research Study 12, *Royal Commission on Criminal Justice* London, HMSO.

Home Office (1995) *The Police and Criminal Evidence Act 1984 (s.66) Codes of Practice B–E,* London, HMSO.

Lyall et al (1995) 'Offending by adults with learning disabilities: identifying need in one health district.' *Mental Handicap Research* 8, 2, pp. 99–109.

Palmer, C,and Hart, M Hart (1996) *'A Pace in the Right Direction? The effectiveness of safeguards in the Police and Criminal Act* Sheffield, Institute for the study of the legal profession, University of Sheffield.

Pearse, J (1995) 'Police Interviewing: The Identification of Vulnerabilities.' *Journal of Community and Applied Psychology*, 5, pp. 147–59.

Philips, Sir C (1981) *The Royal Commission on Criminal Procedure* Report Cmnd 8092, London, HMSO.

Chapter 7
Learning Disabilities:
Recognition and risk

Debra Fearns

People with learning disabilities are, like anyone else, likely to have contact with the police in a number of ways: they may be victims of crime, suspects, or witnesses to a crime. The Criminal Justice System (CJS) in England is not always responsive to the needs and challenges posed by people with learning disabilities, mainly due to a lack of education concerning the issues that may arise when working with people with learning disabilities or those with mental health needs.

There has been a small, yet significant number of cases which has demonstrated some of the difficulties faced by the police in identifying and recognising when a suspect may have a learning disability or mental illness. The Code of Practice to the Act requires that special protection is provided to such a vulnerable suspect, stating that:

> *If an officer has any suspicion, or is told in good faith, that a person of any age may be mentally disordered or mentally handicapped, or mentally incapable of understanding the significance of questions put to him or his replies, then the person shall be treated as a mentally disordered or mentally handicapped person for the purpose of this code.* (Code C, Annex E 1. Page 75)

There have been cases where this did not happen. For example, in the case of Kenny (Crim LR. 284, 1994):

> *the defendant had been arrested for burglary. He had the mental age of a 10 year old. He was interviewed without either a solicitor or an 'appropriate adult' being present, and made admissions. At the trial the Judge allowed in the admissions, not withstanding the obvious breeches. On appeal, the court said this was wrong. The Judge had decided that the admissions were reliable, and had then gone on to decline to exercise his discretion to exclude. Section 76(2) (2) of PACE states that no confession may be relied on, unless the prosecution can prove that it was not obtained as a consequence of anything said or done which was likely in the circumstances existing at the time to render it unreliable. The correct approach would have been to ask whether the failure to have an 'appropriate adult' present rendered the confession likely to be unreliable.* (Bently, 1995)

As stated earlier, one of the most serious difficulties faced by police officers (and of other professionals within the criminal justice sytem) is the difficulty in identifying vulnerable suspects who have a learning disability. How a person is defined as having a learning disability has changed over time; moving from what are now considered to be the crude terms (imbecile, idiot) used in the 1913 Mental Deficiency Act to a more recent shift from the term 'mental handicap' to the term 'learning disability'.

It is estimated that between 2 and 3% of the population have a learning disability. Around 20 people in every thousand will not have all of the skills necessary to lead an independent life, especially at times of crisis. About 3 or 4 people in every thousand have learning disabilities which will require frequent support with aspects of daily living. (Department of Health 1995)

The majority of people in this country who have a mild learning disability are classified as having an intelligence quotient (IQ) measure of between 50 and 70. The average person has an IQ of 100. These individuals will have some degree of intellectual impairment, although the majority may not ever be in contact, or known to, specialist services unless they experience additional difficulties in coping with their environment. Many people with a learning disability adapt to their environments extremely well and live and work in the community in the same way as everyone else.

It should be noted that:

- the term learning disability covers many different conditions and encompasses a wide variety of outcomes for the person concerned

- people with learning disabilities do not form a homogeneous group

- classifying someone as having a learning disability can be dependent on the opinion of one or two individuals

Risk assessment
Problems in identifying predictors.
People who have a learning disability are no more or no less likely than anyone else to be violent or exhibit difficult behaviour; therefore making pre-dictions about a person's likely behaviour can be a dubious business. However, it is obvious that some people will show distress over and above what might be normally expected because of their learning disability, and this distress may show itself in several different ways.

It cannot be assumed that all people who have a common syndrome will react and behave in the same way. Every individual is affected to a different degree, will have had different life experiences, and will therefore show fear and/or anxiety in different ways. People with learning disabilities who are in a highly excitable state may be more dangerous to themselves than to other people. Many people with a learning disability have communication problems, both in understanding other people, and in being understood by other people. Their response may be to 'lash out' at the nearest person, but it is equally likely that such people may 'internalise' their feelings, anger and frustration, and therefore cause harm to themselves, possibly by biting, scratching, head banging or other self-injurious behaviours.

None of this can be accurately predicted but, in assessing such risks, the following should be addressed:

- the person's past history
- the person's state of mind, behaviour and outlook
- discrepancies between what someone says and what that person does
- the person's level of functioning: is behaviour deteriorating/has the person become more voluble/withdrawn?

When dealing with people who have learning disabilities it is also worth considering the following additional points:

- always tell the person what you are doing and why (even if there is no response it does not mean they do not understand.)
- listen to the person and be seen to be listening, even if there are long gaps
- be calm and take your time
- re-phrase your questions if you feel sure the person does not understand what you are saying and use plain, simple language (amplify with signs and/or pictures if you feel it is necessary)
- do not use offensive, derogatory terms such as 'idiot', 'moron' or 'retarded'

One final important point to make is that having a learning disability does not exclude the individual from:

- having committed a crime (and understanding the consequences)
- having committed a crime (without understanding the consequences)
- being a victim of crime

On first appearance it may not be possible to judge whether a person is vulnerable. However, it is always useful to be guided by observing the behaviour of the suspect. If, as the custody process progresses, there is an increasing level of difficulty exhibited by the suspect, it might be worth asking questions. These questions can indicate that steps need to be taken to ensure that interviews are properly conducted within the Codes' requirements for dealing sensitively and effectively with people with learning disabilities, and the need for an Appropriate Adult.

Suggested questions which could be asked

1. What school did you attend?
    (you can then check whether it was a 'mainstream' school or special school)
2. What job do you have?
3. Do you attend college or a day centre?
4. Is there someone we should contact to let them know you're here?
5. How did you get here?
6. Do you receive unemployment or any other kind of benefit?
7. Are you taking any tablets or medicine at the moment?
8. When did you last visit a doctor?
9. Are you visited regularly by a social worker, nurse or other helper?
10. Do you live independently or with other people?
11. Do you require someone to assist you with the police interview?
12. Can you read this form, or do you need assistance?
13. Can you tell me why you are being held in the police station?
14. Can you tell me a bit about yourself?

Common conditions associated with learning disability: Down's Syndrome
Features at birth:
- low birth weight.
- low set ears.
- small mouth.
- flat nasal bridge.
- congenital heart disease (not always present).

Features in adult life
- may be short and stocky in stature.
- pronounced facial features that make the syndrome recognised.

- may have a tendency to have associated sensory defects (for example, be hard of hearing).

- increased tendency to suffer from pre-senile dementia (onset can be as early as in the late thirties)

Incidence
- 1,700 live births.
- maternal age related.

Common difficulties
Some people who have Down's Syndrome may have difficulty in speaking clearly, and in hearing clearly; therefore extra care may need to be taken in attempting to communicate effectively. Equally a person with Down's Syndrome may find complex ideas difficult to understand, and you may need to use very concrete ideas, and use very plain and simple terminology. Typically, they may give answers that they think you want to hear, in an effort to please you.

Autism
Features in childhood and adult life
- lack of response to other people
- delay in the acquisition of speech.
- insistence on the preservation of keeping surrounding environment unchanged
- onset before the age of three years
- Treats people as objects: cannot form a meaningful, reciprocal relationship with family

Common difficulties
- no outward sign that an individual has anything wrong with them.
- effects can be very mild or conversely, very severe.
- do not understand and are unable to use the rules that commonly govern 'normal' behaviour.
- due to their naivety, may be easily led by others around them.
- individuals can display extremes of behaviour if their daily routine is interrupted.
- inappropriateness of visual responses can cause problems: for example, those with autism may smile at everyone they meet, and get into difficulties because of these responses.

Although the police commonly act with tact and understanding, there is still a need for them to learn and understand more about this confusing and alienating impairment.

Tourette's Syndrome
Features in childhood and adult life
- often undiagnosed in childhood and adult life
- characterised by muscular/motor or vocal tics (that is, involuntary rapidly occurring movements or vocal sounds)

Common difficulties
- no outward sign that sufferers have anything wrong with them
- vocal tics can include shouting, screaming, coughing, using expletives (the noises are loud, frightening and language can sometimes be viewed as obscene)
- these voices can appear to other people as rudeness or as threatening, aggressive behaviour
- motor tics can include sufferers hitting themselves, touching themselves (or others), jumping up in the air, suddenly bending down or kicking out, therefore to other people these movements can be frightening
- self-injurious behaviour, such as biting or banging or slapping, has been associated with syndrome
- the person with Tourette's Syndrome may also display inappropriate sexual behaviour such as exposure, or touching other people in sexually inappropriate areas.
- the person with Tourette's Syndrome may feel increasingly frustrated and isolated as other people draw away from her/him through fear

Tourette's Syndrome is a particularly distressing disorder both to the individual concerned and to the general public who know nothing of why such behaviour is occurring. The police need to ensure that they treat the person with tact and understanding and get other professionals (such as nurses and social workers) involved.

References
Bently, (1995) 'PACE Update' *Solicitor's Journal* 27 January.

Department of Health (1995) *Learning Disability: Meeting Needs through Targeting Skills* London, HMSO.

Chapter 8
Juvenile Detainees: One detainee's views
Brian Littlechild

Tony is sixteen years of age and lives in a medium sized town in the South of England. He agreed to talk about his experiences of police detention after discussions with his Youth Offending Team worker and myself. Tony appeared relatively relaxed during our meeting, and recalled that he had been detained on some thirty occasions, mostly in the local area, but also as far away as the South coast and Cambridgeshire. His offences had been varied: criminal damage, shoplifting, burglary of commercial premises and car theft. He was subject to a 2-year supervision order, which specified activities, at the time our meeting took place.

Tony recalled that the first occasion on which the police detained him, it was with friends and relatives of the same age several years ago. He saw this at the time as 'a laugh' They had been arrested for stealing alcohol from shops in the town centre.

He said that, on this occasion, he had been shouting and treating the detention as a joke, and the authority of the police officer as of little consequence. He realised that he could come across to the police in a way that they would see as 'winding them up', as he put it. Tony stated that he was treated very roughly on that occasion; he attributed this to his way of behaving, which would have made the police angry. He said that he was treated roughly and pushed around by certain officers, and that the custody officer had not intervened at this stage as he thought he should have done.

Winding up police and winding up young people
We talked about his relationship with the local police. He said he found some 'coppers', as he referred to them, were very provocative towards him, and would not allow him to walk the streets without calling out through their car windows to him that they were surprised he was still free and not in custody. He said that the good policemen were the ones who treated him with respect. Put simply, this 'respect' seemed to be the way police spoke to him; he accepted they were doing their job as they had to, but he did object to the way some of them carried out their tasks, and their attitude towards him. He thought some policemen could be very macho and that young people could either become aggressive and surly in return, or treat the whole affair as a

joke and make comments that were designed to 'wind-up' the police. He was of the opinion that if there was rough treatment, custody officers tended to choose not to see this, and that police officers would stick together and would not challenge each other if they saw aggressive behaviour from fellow officers. He just accepted that 'this was the way they do it'.

His subsequent experiences in detention, when not detained with such a large group of arrested suspects, were essentially unpleasant. He said that being held in a police station 'does your head in', and that when he was in the cell he just wishes he could get out as soon as possible. He felt very isolated, and at the point at which he was led through the police station and locked away in a cell he wished he had not carried out the action that led to him being detained. He said that sometimes the bell was not answered if he was being held in the cell for a long while, and that he was not allowed to smoke in the cells any more. He said some of the policemen were happy to allow him to come out of the cell to smoke once or twice and to have a cup of tea before the solicitor and Appropriate Adult arrived but others were not.

He said that he found it difficult to know what the reaction of different custody officers would be. Sometimes he would act in a reasonable manner, as he saw it, but could still be treated in a very disrespectful manner by the police. He thought that this depended on the custody officer and the attitude towards their work and young people, but also the mood they were in (for example, as a result of the pressures they were under in their work at that time). He said he thought that some of the policemen believed that they were 'hard'.

He said that he does not listen to his rights when they are read out to him; he thinks this is a way of winding police officers up. He said that he has heard them enough times now, although he did not really take them in when he was first read them. He thought that this was another process to be gone through but that it did not really affect, or could affect, the conditions of detention.

He said that at times the custody officers would throw the piece of paper at him when he was shouting or being 'stroppy', and he believed that this was the reason for the length of wait that he sometimes had for a solicitor or an Appropriate Adult; the police would not make such strenuous efforts to gain attendance as quickly as possible.

Solicitors and Appropriate Adults: differences and similarities
He said that he always asked for a solicitor and he had experienced varying quality over the years, but recently he had found quite a good one. On average, he estimated his wait for the solicitor at about 1–2 hours, whereas

the wait for the Appropriate Adult can be 3–4 hours. In general, he finds the best solicitors spend half an hour talking with the police to find out what has already been obtained in terms of evidence, and then they discuss this with him so that he can decide whether to give a 'no comment' interview or to admit the offence. He said good solicitors tell him what is likely to happen based on their discussions with the police.

He said solicitors who are not so good tend to just sit in the room and say nothing. They will not make efforts to find out the conditions of detention and what has happened before the arrest. He said that the solicitors who tended not to represent him well were the ones who appeared to be fairly friendly with the police. Some solicitors would sit and have a cigarette and a cup of tea with the police officers and this raised some doubts in his mind about how independent and how effective they would be if they had this type of relationship. Tony thought that some Appropriate Adults had the same type of relationship with the police as these solicitors. The importance of the independence of the Appropriate Adult from the police, and the importance of the Appropriate Adult clearly demonstrating this, is a key feature of Appropriate Adults' interventions. This is also shown in the chapters by Debra Fearns and Grethe Hansen which set out the experiences of people with learning disabilities and mental health problems, and in Chapter 11 which sets out the experiences of volunteers in Appropriate Adult schemes.

Tony found that sometimes it appeared that solicitors just wished to 'let things go' so they could get home quickly, and that some of the Appropriate Adults appeared to take this approach as well. He said what was really important for him was that the solicitor, Appropriate Adult or police officer took time to talk to him; this showed him whether they were concerned about him as a person or not. If it did not happen then he did not see how the solicitors could effectively represent him in relation to the crime, as he put it, or how Appropriate Adults could effectively look after his welfare. This was how he saw the differentiation of the roles: the solicitor dealt with the alleged crime, the Appropriate Adult with his welfare.

Experiences of Appropriate Adults
Tony seemed clear about the purpose of the Appropriate Adult role. He said that Appropriate Adults were there to sit and observe what was happening and to make sure that there was no inappropriate behaviour. He had a clear idea about what this inappropriate behaviour could be in terms of repetitive questioning, delayed breaks for refreshments and so on. He was also able to state his

view that the Appropriate Adult should be there to explain what the police are asking and possibly intervene concerning certain types of questioning, and it was not just solicitors who could or should do this.

He said that he had experienced a mixture of people acting as Appropriate Adults: professionals, relatives, and volunteers from a fairly informally organised Appropriate Adult scheme. On one occasion, a friend who was older than him acted as an Appropriate Adult, but he thought that he should not have done so because he was involved in the crime, and they both had to cover this up through the interview. Later his friend was arrested in relation to the crime and for acting as an Appropriate Adult when he should not have done. He said that from amongst his relatives, his mother had acted on the most occasions, his father on several occasions and his grandmother on one occasion.

He said that from amongst the non-relatives who had attended, only on one occasion had the Appropriate Adult sat down in private with him before the interview to check that he had been treated well, and to spend some time explaining the Appropriate Adult's role.

He said he was not concerned about the age or gender of an Appropriate Adult, only that they would take time to 'chat' to him, to make a connection to enable him to trust that they are concerned about him and looking after his welfare.

He said that the police had always attempted to contact his first choice of Appropriate Adult. Normally, his criterion was the one who could get there with the least delay so that he could leave the police station as quickly as possible.

Relatives as Appropriate Adults

His mother has been called to the police station the greatest number of times during the past few years, and she had learnt that she could challenge the police. He described her as being assertive, and she would intervene if she thought the police were being aggressive. He did say that his mother had become very upset and angry with him at times, if she learnt he had been arrested by the police again. He said that she shouts at him, and that she had done this in the cell before the interview had started, and then during the interview as well. His grandmother when she had attended did not know what to do, so could not represent him; she would just sit there and this did not feel supportive. His father, when he had attended on a few occasions, had also objected to police behaviour at times.

84

He said that on one occasion it had been distressing for him because his mother had started to intervene during which she gave some details about his movements at the time of the alleged offence, which he believed had effectively incriminated him. He said that he had been very upset about this and that he had stopped speaking to her for a period of time afterwards. He said that this had also been, amongst others, one of the reasons why he had left home at that point. He said that neither his mother nor his father had abused him physically while they were angry that he had been arrested, but he did say that his mother in particular had been verbally and emotionally abusive towards him. He said that she had now stopped coming out to him and that it was normally the Youth Offending Team workers or the volunteers from the informal Appropriate Adult Scheme who attended.

Due to the family relationship issues involved, he said that on one occasion when he was a long way from home following his arrest for the theft of a car, he particularly asked for an Appropriate Adult who was not a relative. He requested this in order to try to ensure that his parents would not be aware of the situation and so would not become angry with him.

It does appear from Tony's experiences that certain parents acting as Appropriate Adults can have significant negative effects on the legal rights and welfare of the young person in custody, and on the subsequent relationships and attitudes within the family.

What does a good Appropriate Adult do?
Tony had experienced that he had always been given a choice of Appropriate Adult. Given his experiences, and what we know from the research concerning the ways in which parents sometimes react towards young people in a judgemental and angry way (Evans, 1993; Brown, 1997), it appears that it may be important that a choice of Appropriate Adult is given to young people (as had happened for Tony), and that there is not seen to be a priority list where a relative should be called first and another type of Appropriate Adult second. This is also important in relation to the experience and knowledge of the Appropriate Adult in carrying out the role, as relatives are very likely to have no training or knowledge of the criminal justice process. In addition, the emotions surrounding the detention can have a negative effect on whether the parents can perform the role effectively. Tony reiterated a number of times that a good Appropriate Adult would spend time talking to him, to make sure they knew how he was feeling at the time. They would also demonstrate an

interest in how he was experiencing the conditions of detention, and make clear to him that they were there for his welfare. Good ones would demonstrate to him that they had a good knowledge of the role and what they should be doing by communicating this to him. In addition, he said, the good Appropriate Adult would intervene if there were oppressive questioning, and that this had happened for him in the past. He said that he liked to have both a solicitor and Appropriate Adult present as it made him feel safer to have two people looking after his interests, even if it was in different ways.

Whilst he knew that the Youth Offending Team workers are paid for their work, he did not seem sure whether the volunteers from the informal Appropriate Adult Scheme were paid. As discussed in Chapter 10, the fact that the volunteers do not get paid, and are not involved in the other areas of work which social workers and Youth Offending Team workers become involved in, made the carrying-out of the role easier and clearer. Tony was clear that some social workers/Youth Offending Team workers were very good in the role whereas others did not focus on the Appropriate Adult role itself, becoming more interested in other areas which they could have responsibility for, so therefore were too 'nosy' in trying to find out and discuss other matters which were not relevant to the immediate detention. Tony realised that this was because they had additional areas of responsibility, whereas Appropriate Adults who were not employed in this capacity could focus clearly on the Appropriate Adult role and did not confuse matters. He had a definite impression that social workers/Youth Offending Team workers interfered in families and could destroy them and had a clear impression of them being too 'nosy' and interfering. He was very concerned about who had access to his files and previous history; social workers, or Youth Offending Team workers access to these was a real concern to him. He felt safer with volunteers who do not have to access to these files.

Experience of detention

Tony said that his interviews had lasted for periods between a few minutes and 5–6 hours. In relation to interviewing techniques, he had on several occasions experienced repetitive questioning where the same type of question was put ten or more times. He also said that the police try to 'trick' young people by asking about events in different ways and trying to catch them out in different events in the story. The message came across strongly from him that, at times, it could be lonely and isolating and that detainees need protection.

On the other hand, there are elements within the situation which can lead young people to be evasive, to try to wind up the police officers, and of there being elements of game-playing within the situation, concerning who would come out on top. He saw this as creating difficulties for those acting in the official roles surrounding this, because of the feelings that could be generated in those who are providing the service, be they a police officer or an Appropriate Adult. He commented on how persistently replying 'no comment', 'no comment', would make the police angry and they may then start to raise their voices and become angry.

He said the presence of Appropriate Adults was particularly important for those who had no family to call on and this it was really important to have them there. In relation to the police, Tony thought that the police could 'sort out their attitude a bit' so that they would not appear so aggressive, become so wound up and not give young people so much 'hassle'.

The main points arising from the meeting with Tony about his experiences are:

- the need for respect for the young person

- communication from officers and Appropriate Adults that they are concerned about the young person's welfare as well as the investigation of the offence

- the Appropriate Adult should take time to talk with the young person and communicate with the young person that they know what they are doing there as the Appropriate Adult, and that they are not just wanting to get away and get back to bed or whatever they were doing before they arrived

- appreciation of the young person's desire to get out of the police station as soon as possible, and how this might affect the process and subsequent outcomes

- the ambivalent feelings young people may have about vulnerability and trying to wind up the police

- the importance of realising the ambivalent relationship of relatives who act as Appropriate Adults, how the relatives may be experiencing it, and how the young person may be experiencing their involvement and the other effects of them being arrested and the effects on the family, which may affect their vulnerability

References
Brown, D (1997) *PACE 10 years on: a review of research* Home Office Research and Statistics Directorate in Research Findings No 49. London, HMSO.

Evans, R (1993) 'Getting Things Taped' *Community Care* November 19.

Chapter 9
Appropriate Adults and Juveniles

Brian Littlechild

The greatest demand on Appropriate Adult services usually arise from the detention of juvenile suspects, although the most severe miscarriages of justice have taken place in relation to vulnerable adults (see Chapter 2). There are not the same problems of recognition as there are for vulnerable adults, but there are particular problems for juveniles in relation to who acts as the Appropriate Adult, and in what ways.

After many years of concern about the treatment of juveniles held in detention for police questioning, the Labour Government issued a Consultation Paper, *New national and local focus on Youth Crime*, in 1997, which recommended that local authorities should be required to ensure Appropriate Adults are available to attend police interviews with juveniles, though this did not include the same provision for vulnerable adults. This was transformed into a requirement in s.38(4)(a) of the Crime and Disorder Act 1998, and is now contained within the *National Standards for Youth Justice*. The latter states that Youth Offending Team managers 'must ensure that appropriate adults can be provided to police stations in their area', and that 'staff or accredited volunteers who act as appropriate adults are trained and supported in this role, and that they are provided with a copy of the PACE Codes of Practice' (Youth Justice Board, 2000:9). The Standards also state that 'parents or primary carers must be encouraged to be present unless there are special circumstances that make this inappropriate' (Youth Justice Board, 2000:9). However, we know that problems frequently exist where professionals fail to carry out the role adequately, which highlights the need for training of non-relative Appropriate Adults (Pierpoint, 1999). In this chapter, I will argue that at times a properly trained and supported Appropriate Adult who is not a relative needs to be in attendance to safeguard the welfare and legal rights of the young person if the relative is unable to carry out the role as the Codes require, in addition to (or instead of) the parent or primary carer.

Inappropriate Appropriate Adults
We know that juveniles may feel under great pressure from parents to 'own up' to an offence, in addition to pressure the young person often feels to gain release from the police station to stop the discomfort and difficulties there and then. Professor Roger Evans found in his research for the Royal

Commission on Criminal Justice in 1993 that whilst many made no contribution at all, of Appropriate Adults who were non-professionals,

> *those that spoke were as likely to be unsupportive of the children in their care. when parents colluded with the police in trying to obtain a confession, they frequently used abusive or oppressive techniques reminiscent of the worst police practices.* (Evans, 1993a)

If this is the case then it can be argued that they are not appropriate Appropriate Adults. The main roles of the Appropriate Adult as far as the criminal justice system is concerned are to facilitate communication between the police and the young person, and to look after the young person's interests and welfare in a general sense.

The concerns about relatives intervening and their methods of doing so are highlighted in the case of *R. v. Jefferson* 1994 (All England Law Review, 270) where the Appropriate Adult was the father. Whilst he intervened on the side of the police, and often contradicted the child's account, the boy's eventual confession of riot and violent behaviour was allowed to stand by the court of Appeal. This means that it is possible for such evidence to be admissible where this has happened, although other case law suggests the opposite. For example, in the case of *R. v. Morse and others* in 1991 (Criminal Law Review 195, 1991), the judge found that an Appropriate Adult who is unable to discharge any or all the duties attributable to the role is an inappropriate choice and puts the interviewee at a disadvantage. This is supported by the findings in the case of the *Director of Public Prosecutions v. Blake* in the Court of Appeal, 30 November 1988 (World Law Review 432, 89 Criminal Appeal Review, 179) where the sixteen-year-old defendant was estranged from her father and living by choice in a hostel for homeless women. She was arrested on suspicion of arson and held for interview. Police asked for her father's address (from which she had previously run away) so he could act as the Appropriate Adult. The young woman refused and made it clear that she would object to his presence; she asked for her social worker. The social worker, in accordance with their employer's local policy, would not attend unless it was impossible to contact any other suitable person or if all others refused to attend. The social worker refused to attend, as the father was prepared to. Eventually the young woman provided the address of her father and he attended. His only words to the defendant were 'Are you alright?' to which she did not reply. During the interview she made a full confession. The interview evidence was later held to be inadmissible because of the obvious inappropriateness of the father's attendance. The justices held that the estranged father was not an appropriate Appropriate Adult, and that the defendant had not been advised by an independent person. They ruled the confession inadmissible under s.76(2)(b) of PACE. There had been no other evidence and the charge was dismissed. The Director of Public Prosecutions appealed but it was held on Appeal that the Appropriate Adult had an important part to play to advise, observe for fairness and, if necessary, help if any problem of communication arose. The Appropriate Adult should not be someone with whom the juvenile had no empathy, or who could not fulfil the objectives of ensuring a fair interview. The Court hoped that:

social workers, on learning of this problem, will take note and relax whatever policy they have so as to ensure that an appropriate adult, in the form of one of their representatives will attend as promptly as practicable at an interview when requested to do so. There is no point in the police officer seeking to protect a juvenile by persistently taking steps to facilitate the attendance, parent or otherwise, whom the juvenile has made it plain he, or she, does not want present.

Subsequently, a new element of the 1991 Codes made clear that estranged parents are not appropriate for use in this role.

It can be argued that one of the reasons that parents or primary carers may not be Appropriate Adults, as suggested by the Youth Justice Board and quoted at the beginning of this chapter (Youth Justice Board, 2000:9), is that they are not able to undertake the role appropriately as in the case of the *Director of Public Prosecutions v. Blake*. There are a number of other High Court and Court of Appeal decisions where the cases have been dismissed because of this. I have argued elsewhere that the use of parents inappropriately to meet the young person's needs in relation to police detention and interviews could be seen as a breach of Article 3(1) of the UN Convention on the Rights of the Child. This requires that the best interests of the child should be the primary consideration in all actions affecting children (Littlechild, 1997, 1998). S.1 of the Children Act also requires agencies to have the child's welfare as a primary consideration. It would be better for Youth Offending Teams and the police to have guidance that when this happens, a youth Offending Team Appropriate Adult should be present.

The Detention and Interviewing of Juveniles: Recent Findings
Brown *et al.'s* study *PACE 10 years on: a review of research* (Home Office, 1997), reviewed what developments there had been as a result of the findings

and recommendations of the 1993 Royal Commission on Criminal Justice. The study found that one-fifth of suspects are juveniles, and the parents usually act as Appropriate Adults, although social workers attend in around one-third of cases. It concluded that it is likely that neither parents nor social workers will have knowledge of police procedures, while parents are in addition often distraught at the child's arrest. Neither plays a significant part in police interviews. Juveniles are less likely than adults to be given full information about their rights and are less likely to seek legal advice. They are more likely than adults to provide confessions.

Findings from Brown *et al.*'s study show that juveniles are less likely than adults to be given full information about their rights, less likely to seek legal advice and more likely than adults to provide confessions. It is particularly worrying therefore that he found that despite PACE having led to a reduction in the frequency of interviews and use of unacceptable interview tactics, the confession rate has changed little, remaining at around 60 per cent. It was also found that some forms of questioning raise concerns about the potential for false confessions; identifying those most prone to make such confessions continues to be problematic; and little supervision or monitoring of interviews occurs despite the ready availability of interview tapes. Some unregulated interviewing continues to occur outside the interview room either on the way to the station or in police cells. It appears that audio-taping has reduced disputes in court about what was said in the interviews as well as stimulating the flow of questioning, which is to be welcomed.

Failure to act on the evidence

The problems demonstrated in the case law and research were highlighted by the 1993 Royal Commission, and they called for a full review of the qualifications, availability and role of the Appropriate Adult. The subsequent consultation by the Home Office concerning a Working Group to be set up in response to the Royal Commission recommended changes ignored submissions to them concerning the issue of parents failing to fulfil the role. This may in part have been due to confusion concerning the concept of parental responsibility, which is central to the Children Act 1989, and how this relates to the individual rights of the child. It also ignored the problem of how Appropriate Adults could be effectively apprised of their role. One submission recommended a notice setting out the role to be signed by the Appropriate Adult, and detainee, to say they understood it, and for a requirement for an independent Appropriate Adult to be called where parents were apparently not carrying out the role. The police training manual from their

Central Planning and Training Unit in 1992 stated that:

> *there should be no doubt in anybody's mind about the role of the Appropriate Adult, they should be briefed prior to the interview. Then when they are introduced during the interview they should be able to explain their responsibilities while the tape is running. (quoted in Evans, 1993b)*

However, this is still often not carried out properly. In any event, the Working Group's considerations were ignored (Pearse and Gudjonsson, 1996a)

In ignoring the rights of children in this way, especially given the new right of courts to infer guilt where a young person has exercised his or her right to silence under the 1994 Criminal Justice and Public Order Act, this inevitably places greater pressure on young people, and increases the possibility of unreliable confessions.

A number of the problems associated with untrained and unsupported Appropriate Adult became evident in the case of Janet Leach, a worker in a young homelessness project in Gloucestershire, when she was called upon to act as a Appropriate Adult for Frederick West in 1994. She subsequently sued the Gloucester police force for compensation, claiming that she was neither prepared properly for the role, nor for what her involvement in such a harrowing set of allegations surrounding the horrendous crimes would mean. In addition, she claimed the police should have assessed her competence and suitability for the role, and that she was told by the police that would not have to give evidence in court, which she subsequently did have to do. These claims were dismissed in a Court of Appeal judgement in July 1998 (Times Law Report, 4 September 1998), but her claims of negligence and breach of duty of care on the police's part when they failed to offer her counselling to aid her with the stress placed upon her by her involvement were allowed to proceed. This raises a number of serious issues about training, preparation and support for Appropriate Adults who are not also relatives. The Appropriate Adult was described by the defence QC as an 'unmitigated disaster', and the court heard submissions which challenged her integrity (Pearse and Gudjonsson, 1996b).

The continuing (in)effectiveness of Appropriate Adult procedures
Research from the Home Office also casts doubt on the effectiveness of Appropriate Adult provision, regarding not only the non-professionals but also the professionals. This again supports the findings of Evans's study where 62 per cent of cases where social workers – mostly residential and youth workers – attended,

police used 'persuasive' tactics to obtain a confession although paragraph 11.3 of Code C specifically precludes this. In addition, in a number of cases police cautioned the young person even where there was no clear admission of any offence on the tape with the Appropriate Adult's agreement (Evans ,1993b).

The role of the Appropriate Adult and the understanding of this by the young person and others involved, is addressed by Brown *et al.* (1993), who found that:

> *observation generally and interviews by observers with parents and juveniles confirm the view that in many cases parents are ill-equipped to fulfil the function envisaged by the Codes. Few Appropriate Adults appear to have much knowledge of police procedures or the law. Some were nervous or subdued at being in a police station and it is unlikely that they took any active part in interviews. Some ... appeared to be strongly on the police's side ... and others fell into completely the opposite and vehemently took sides against the police.*

This is hardly a facilitation of communication and these are occasions when it is unsuitable for the parent/guardian to act as the Appropriate Adult.

As a result of this knowledge, and the needs of the young people and the criminal justice system, it may be that where the carer or parent is not carrying out their role properly the social worker or someone else from some from an approved Appropriate Adult scheme should be called to ensure the role is carried out appropriately, with the proper training and support which they should have.

Summary of main points
- the Appropriate Adult must be able to be seen to have engaged with the detainee, and at the very least not have such a poor relationship with them that this could be seen to affect the interview and any evidence gained from it

- police may need to consider if a relative may be an inappropriate choice, and an Appropriate Adult from an agency or scheme needs to be called in addition to the relative

- Appropriate Adults should be confident in their role, and in the back-up from any scheme or employer in any difficulties which might arise

References
Brown, D, Ellis, T and Larcombe, K (1993) *Changing the Code: police detention under the revised PACE Codes of Practice* Home Office Research Study 129, London, HMSO

Evans, R (1993a) 'The conduct of Police Interviews with Juveniles' *Research Study No. 8. The Royal Commission on Criminal Justice* London, HMSO.

Evans, R (1993b) 'Getting Things Taped' *Community Care* 19 November.

Littlechild, B (1997) 'Young Offenders, Punitive Policies and the Rights of children' *Critical Social Policy* 17(4), pp. 73–92.

Littlechild, B (1998) 'An end to Inappropriate Adults?' *Childright* 144 (April) pp.5–7.

Pearse, J and Gudjonsson, G (1996a) 'How appropriate are Appropriate Adults?' *Journal of Forensic Psychiatry* 7(3) pp. 570–80.

Pearse, J and Gudjonsson, G (1996b)'Understanding the problems of the Appropriate Adult' *Expert Evidence* 4(3), pp. 101–4.

Pierpoint, H (1999) 'Appropriate Practice? Young suspects' Rights Under the UNCRC' *Childright* 162 (December), pp. 8–11.

Youth Justice Board (2000) *National Standards for Youth Justice* London, Youth justice Board.

Chapter 10
The Police Experience of Appropriate Adult Volunteers

Keith Baldwin

Introduction

My main aim in producing this short chapter is to present some experiences of custody sergeants who have dealt with vulnerable detainees requiring the services of an Appropriate Adult on a regular basis. A number of issues are raised concerning the need for police to identify vulnerable suspects as defined by the Police and Criminal Evidence 1984 Code of Practice section C, and to secure the attendance of Appropriate Adults.

The chapter was prepared with the help of some sergeants in the Hertfordshire constabulary, namely Emma Balser, Gary Richards and Jim Binyon, and we met in order to examine what police officers have found is good and useful in Appropriate Adult provision. We also reviewed what has been found to be unhelpful and problematical for the police and suspects in the way that the legislative demands relating to Appropriate Adults are operationalised. The sergeants felt that in essence they had been given an ad hoc and loosely structured system to operate, and it took their best efforts to make the system work.

Family members as Appropriate Adults

With regard to using family members as Appropriate Adults for alleged juvenile offenders, the problems were many and varied. There was also a distinct difference between the attitude displayed by the family members of those being detained for the first time and those of young people with a greater level of exposure to the criminal justice system. On their first visit to a police station, family members were likely to listen attentively to the requirements of the police and to take an active and generally unbiased role in the proceedings. That said, much always depended upon the previous experiences of the parents or guardians, in that those who had themselves been arrested previously were far more likely to be less than impartial. These adults would then intervene in ways which related more to their own views of the police rather than trying to act in an impartial way and aid communication as the Appropriate Adult role requires.

Difficulties could also be encountered by single parents who are unable to attend as they would wish because of child care responsibilities, and also with parents or guardians who are at work when the juveniles in their care have been detained during working hours. The need for parents or guardians

– or even older siblings – to bring young children with them (sometimes even babes in arms) is also a developing trend. To deal with this, some custody stations now maintain their own stock of toys with which to entertain these young children. Additionally, the provision of transport to get family members to and from the police station is problematical, especially where contact has to be made via another police area because the home address is located in another part of the county, or even another part of the country.

Overall the sergeants felt that those who did attend as Appropriate Adults generally took matters seriously, but seemed largely to adopt a passive stance of observer and countersignatory. Additionally, the 'appropriateness' of some adult family members could be called into question. Occasions had even existed where some Appropriate Adults had themselves required Appropriate Adult support at times when they had been detained on previous occasions. Parents or guardians who could not read or write and members of minority ethnic communities who had language difficulties posed their own unique problems. The sergeants reported that although every consideration would be given to the appropriateness of the adults concerned, there was always a pressure to overcome the delay factor and to go ahead in spite of some of the inadequacies mentioned above.

Dealys to justice
The effects of these different problems frequently culminate in extensive delays to the judicial process. On many occasions the officer in the case had spent a good deal of time trying to negotiate the attendance of an Appropriate Adult. This was to the detriment of interview preparation and the collation of evidence concerning the case for which the person had been detained. It was not uncommon for alleged offenders to be bailed on more than one occasion rather than keep them detained at the police station for undue periods of time. An example was given of one offender (arrested for taking a conveyance without consent) who had been bailed 5 times and had spent 8 hours in detention without the investigation making any progress. This makes clear the importance of having arrangements in place that can ensure the attendance of an Appropriate Adult at the earliest opportunity.

Local Appropriate Adult services
So far as Appropriate Adults from a countywide list maintained by Social Services was concerned, the sergeants reported a general theme of good support during office hours, but distinct problems in getting adequate responses at night time or weekends. Some Divisions had as many as 100

names on volunteer lists where others only had a few. In addition, some Divisions paid token expenses of about £5, while others paid nothing. It seemed that in many instances a small number of highly committed volunteers would attend time and again rather than leave the police and the detained person without any support.

A significant problem area for the custody sergeants related to the identification of detained persons who might have a mental disorder or varying levels of learning difficulties. The ability to recognise signs and symptoms and the need to ask appropriate questions was considered to be a continuing training requirement (these issues are dealt with in Chapters 5, 6 and 7). This situation was often complicated by the circumstances of the arrest where the detained person could have been exhibiting strange behaviour due to drink, drugs or the display of anger/aggression.

The above comments relate very generally to a fairly complex, but vitally important element within the criminal justice process on which work seems to be needed to produce a more sophisticated, coherent and robust system. The sergeants felt that an answer may partly lie in setting up central detention units or 'Bridewell' facilities perhaps two in number for a county such as Hertfordshire with its million population, where full-time or dedicated staff (which could include medical and nursing support) may be better able to deal with this element of the system.

Chapter 11
Good Schemes, Good Services: Experiences of
Appropriate Adult Volunteers

Brian Littlechild

The aim of this chapter is to explore the experiences and views of Appropriate Adults who have worked as part of two successful schemes, one for young people provided by NCH Action for Children, and the other for vulnerable adults organised by Southampton MIND. The important aspects of developing such schemes are set out by Andrew Strong, the manager of the MIND scheme, in Chapter 12.

The meetings with the Appropriate Adults from both schemes were based upon an open-ended semi-structured interview schedule, in order to allow the participants to raise the issues they had recognised and dealt with. Questions were used as prompts only to ensure the main themes of this book were addressed, covering issues involving their experience of the work with the suspects, the police and the organisation they worked for. In both situations the purpose of publication was explained, and that those interviewed would not be personally identified in the book. All the participants were sent transcripts of the draft chapter in order to suggest amendments and corrections, which were then taken into account in the final version. They were very willing to give their time to explain their work as one way of improving understanding of the role and the schemes.

Southampton NCH Action for Children Appropriate Adult Scheme
At NCH Action for Children, the Appropriate Adults took part in a group session discussing their work following a training event.

No fewer than seventeen of the volunteers in this scheme had agreed to take part in the group discussion focused on an examination of their experiences of carrying out the role. The people who are volunteers come from very varied backgrounds. There are a number of people who are in employment, a number of people who are unemployed at present, and a number of people who are retired.

The volunteers were enthusiastic about discussing their experiences and views. They obviously had a real commitment to representing young people and being able to help maintain the young people's dignity and respect within a setting that can easily disempower. As might be expected from a group of people who had been recruited specifically for this purpose, they had energy and a keen interest in ensuring they carried out their tasks well on behalf of the scheme itself and for the young people who are detained. The volunteers demonstrated an appreciation of the job that the police had to do, but had a clear focus on their Appropriate Adult role and duties, and its importance.

Experiences of acting as an Appropriate Adult

A number of the volunteers discussed how they had become more confident over time in carrying out the role and it was obviously important for them to be able to share their experiences and discuss how they could handle difficult situations in group meetings arranged regularly by the manager. The importance of having a co-ordinator or manager to whom they can go with difficult problems in relation to particular suspects, police officers or situations in order to be given help to work out how to best deal with them was made clear. The ability and willingness of the manager to be able to pick up general themes and problems so as to be able to represent these and facilitate change where needed (with, for example, police representatives on steering groups) was also highlighted.

The participants believed it was important to feel confident in how they related to the police officers. They perceived a need for an amicable relationship, but also knew they had to be assertive at times, and to know how to challenge police behaviour when it is seemingly pressuring the suspect. They clearly saw their role as that of an advocate for the interests of the suspects.

The participants talked of the importance of making a relationship with the young person even if it was to be only a brief one. A number spoke of how important it is to demonstrate their interest and concern for the young person, which can help enormously in putting them at their ease in what can often be a very difficult situation. One theme which emerged from the discussion was that the clear focus of their role as volunteers in undertaking the Appropriate Adult functions appeared to allow a better relationship with the young person than if it was their social worker, or indeed any social worker, who was there in the interview. This was seen to be because the social workers had other agendas which they had to have regard to in relation to their agency function and responsibilities for the young person. These complicating and sometimes confounding factors for social workers appeared to the group of volunteers to be helpfully omitted when they undertook the role. This meant that the young person knew that the volunteer was only focusing on them and their situation and needs at that time, rather than having other roles, demands and sets of relationships to think about as well, as a social worker would often have to do.

This could be an important feature for those organising schemes to bear in mind when setting up their services and developing them.

When asked about what they found helpful for themselves and the young people in interviewing officers' and custody officers' approaches, the main elements would seem to be that the officers spoke and dealt with the young people and the Appropriate Adult in a way which showed concern and respect. This has been a consistent finding in caring professions research over decades: treating people with respect and valuing them, no matter what they have done or the difficulties they may be in, is important.

Some of the volunteers did find that some of the interviewing officers were more skilled and sensitive in their approaches than others. They also found that there might be some differences between interviewing officers when young people decided that they wished to make no comments in answer to questions or in relation to perceived disinterest/disengagement in the suspect. Most of the volunteers said that if they saw oppressive behaviour, of which they seemed to have a reasonable understanding, they knew how to intervene and would intervene, even though they might feel uncomfortable about this. The participants were confident that they would be assertive about securing a private session with the young person before going into the interview proper, and knew that they could do this. They saw this as important in setting up the relationship with the suspect.

In the main they found custody officers helpful and knowledgeable. Most believed they went often enough to get to know the custody officers, which is valuable. However, there were some participants who found particular custody officers difficult. With those custody officers whom they found difficult, they believed that this may have been due to the views of the custody officer about the Appropriate Adult carrying out their role properly. This might include such things as ensuring they took time with the suspect, that the suspect understood everything, and all went according to the book. As the Appropriate Adults see it, this could cause some friction and difficulties. This was very much the exception to the rule in their experience, however.

Relationships with other agencies
The Steering Groups are an important forum in which to discuss problems raised by volunteers, but the manager at the NCH Action for Children scheme said that attendance at the steering group was not as regular as it had been, as the agencies' representatives felt that arrangements were satisfactory.

Also, there had been occasions when after the scheme had run well for a year, the police had asked for a volunteer to go out, and later telephoned before the Appropriate Adult's arrival to say there was not enough evidence to proceed. This raises issues for discussion with the police representatives on Steering Groups concerning their expectations about when the volunteers should be called, as it seemed that this was being used almost as an insurance policy.

Another issue raised was requirement to attend, if for example, it is a situation in which a female volunteer is asked to attend where the accused is held for serious sexual offences; or where they know the detainee in another way. In addition to this, what expectations should the contracting department, if this is a Youth Offending Team or Social Services, have concerning volunteers attending at all times for all cases?

One of the issues that arose with such contracting agencies was the relationship with other providers of Appropriate Adult services, particularly emergency duty teams. This might raise issues concerning expectations on when the volunteers should attend; so, for example, if it is a particular situation as described above which is particularly difficult for the volunteer in some way, should they as volunteers have the right not to attend? This is a question of protocol that schemes may wish to ensure is in place, which may need to be discussed with others on the steering group or senior police officers, concerning the limits and boundaries relating to when volunteer Appropriate Adults attend, and when others should attend.

One of the issues that may emerge from this is the knowledge we have of the outcomes where someone who is not within an agency structure, such as the non-statutory agency employee who attended in the Fred West case. The person contacted there did not feel that she was properly briefed about what she was undertaking, what she would be hearing, how long it would take, and the effects it might have on her emotionally. She was subsequently criticised by the defence lawyer for her actions (for further discussion of this situation, see chapter 9).

Experiences of legal representation were also in the main quite good but some representatives were perceived to be variable in terms of their helpfulness and commitment to the young person.

Summary
In the main, the volunteers saw themselves as advocates for the young people and for ensuring that their rights and interests were maintained. They had a very clear focus on this, and what it entailed. The importance of having

training sessions and individual support from the manager was clear and the cohesion of those working together on this clearly focused goal, which is not always possible for social workers, became clear during the session. They had no other distractions in their role and could focus on the young person, and this seemed to produce the positive effects which the government (through the provision of the Codes) had hoped for from the Appropriate Adult role, and for the young people themselves.

Most of the volunteers said they did it because they enjoyed working with young people in the setting of the police detention. They felt that they were providing a valuable service, and that their presence and interventions had a real effect on the situation at the time.

Southampton MIND
At Southampton MIND, interviews took place with two Appropriate Adults. David had been an Appropriate Adult for over 5 years, carrying out over 150 Appropriate Adult interviews. He had recently had a 2-year break from the work before returning to the scheme. Ron was relatively new to the scheme. (I have not used their real names.)

Experiences of acting as an Appropriate Adult
I asked a general question about relationships with the police, and they said they found the police were on the whole helpful. However, with both police and solicitors they believed it was important not to be manipulated by them, or to be seen by suspects to appear to be manipulated by them. They also said that at times they can feel that they have limited opportunities for representing suspects within the capacity afforded by the role; this means that on occasions they cannot always help clients as much they would wish. These situations seemed to relate more to general welfare issues for clients/suspects than the criminal investigation process *per se*.

Ron said as a new volunteer he had initially found it a problem establishing himself in the charge room, and even getting through the door into the station; this has been an issue raised by social workers on many training courses led by the author. Ron said that sometimes the police do not take the Appropriate Adult volunteers as seriously as they should since the police do need them to perform this important function properly.

Both Ron and David said that it was difficult at times to find somewhere to sit quietly to examine custody records properly, and these were sometimes very long and complex. The issue of space was obviously an important one physically, but also in terms of establishing oneself within the set of dynamics which determined who was driving events. They clearly felt that at times the police were seeing themselves in complete control, and were not sensitive enough to the problems and needs of vulnerable adults. They believed the police are much more familiar with dealing with suspects who are not vulnerable, and that it is sometimes easy to get caught in the police 'tramlines' of processes and procedures which are not sensitive to a vulnerable suspect's needs.

The importance of independence

The Southampton MIND, and also the NCH Action for Children Appropriate Adults found that it was important they made it clear to the police and the suspects that they are independent of, and different from, everyone else who may attend, such as lay visitors, solicitors and social services staff, a point noted by Pearse and Gudjonsson (1996). This sometimes took suspects by surprise and they took some while to appreciate that the Appropriate Adult was there to be a supporter to them. This was an alien concept to most suspects unless they had previous experience of an Appropriate Adult. However, Ron felt that sometimes suspects could be somewhat dismissive of Appropriate Adults when they discovered they had no power as such. David was clear that having spelt out the role to the suspect, and having made clear his concern for the welfare of the person, that this made an enormous difference for suspects. Both also believed it was important to explore whether the suspect had received refreshments and meals appropriately, as the codes required; this, importantly, demonstrated practical concern to the suspect.

David described how he thought the suspects experienced their detentions. If they had not had experience of detention before, and sometimes even if they had, they were stripped of their dignity and were often traumatised by things being taken away from them and being (literally) banged away in a cell. It was clear that the focus on their welfare afforded by the attention of the Appropriate Adult was in their view extremely important for suspects. David stated that he thought it was important that he consider whether a Forensic Medical Examiner (FME, previously known as a police surgeon) was needed; for example, if suspects were suffering from problems because they did not have their medication. He also thought it was important to ascertain if there were any other inter-agency links: for example, if the suspect was currently known to health and/or social care professionals. If suspects are known to other agencies, there may need to be contact with those agencies if this could gain valuable information on the suspect's mental health and emotional state, provided the suspect agrees.

David gave an example of where the lack of power and control inherent in the role had actually been valuable for all concerned. He talked of how there were three large police officers outside a cell with a man inside whom David had known before. The man had been aggressive but David was able to persuade the police officers to let him speak with the man, and for a woman custody officer to bring the man a mug of tea. He had then been able to transfer the suspect's feelings of trust towards David himself to the woman custody officer who had brought the tea. He also talked about how he had mediated on other occasions. In one situation a woman had been handcuffed, and when released she had become very agitated and violent. He had spoken to her boyfriend who was outside, and told him he would see that she was safe. The boyfriend was able to calm down after he had also started to become agitated. He said that both the boyfriend and the suspect accepted his role and he was able to calm matters as he was not part of the power relationships and 'stand offs' which inevitably come about in those type of situations. It is to be remembered, though, that David was very experienced in the role.

David described how, at times, if the FME said clearly that the person was unable to proceed because of lack of medication or because of particular problems, the police would use PACE s.47(3)(a) bail, and ask the suspect to report again. David said he became concerned about this as the person might hear voices saying he should not turn up again, and had arrived early one day when this had happened to ensure the person would arrive at the police station, which he fortunately had. He thinks that custody officers should be trained to ask when someone is received into the custody suite whether they have medical problems and whether they have any medicines about their person, or are in need of any. From his experience, this does not usually happen.

The police role
Both Ron and David could appreciate the difficulties for police officers carrying out their roles, and that they could become very stressed with the number of people they had to deal with at times, and the types of problems those people with vulnerabilities presented them with. They knew that this could make them sometimes less sensitive in their responses, and that these were probably defensive reactions to trying to cope with their job and getting through to the end of their shift. They thought that sometimes custody officers must feel it difficult to be able to come back to work the next day after some of the difficult shifts they had seen them having to manage.

They were clear that the police did always read out the role of the Appropriate Adult and the rights of the person. However, they were concerned that suspects often did not really understand the role until the Appropriate Adult took the time to meet in private with them and explain it fully.

They were also concerned about the stresses on suspects. They thought this affected suspects' behaviour more than anything else, and good custody officers were aware of this and did their best to ameliorate the effects. It was clear for those with mental health problems that they attended for, that suspects would often say 'I just want to get out' and will waive their rights to a solicitor, or whatever else, in order just to be free. This is confirmed by a number of other reported experiences detailed in chapters five and eight of this book, and the reasons for the Appropriate Adult role being in place. They did however think that there are some officers who are provocative in the things they say, for example 'Are you here for the nutters?' David dealt with this by having a quiet word with the officer rather than making a complaint.

Good custody officers could be sensitive to the possible problems and needs of those in the vulnerable groups, whereas the poorer custody officers and and/or those under stress had difficulty in changing gear from dealing with "villains" to "vulnerability". They both found that the transfer of custody officers at the end of shifts was a problem because a significant change of approach could occur. They had been required to try to smooth this process through on a number of occasions.

They said that the good custody officers allowed time and space for things to happen properly, and for the Appropriate Adult to form a trust relationship with the client/suspect. David thought it was important to be vigilant for police officers who have pet hates of particular crimes, for example shop lifting, burglary or whatever else this may be.

Support for the Appropriate Adult
David thought it was particularly important to make sure that the Appropriate Adult knows of the safety measures in place, such as where the bells are and how to summon support very quickly in case there was a problem. He seemed to feel quite secure with this, whereas Ron, who was relatively new to the scheme, was still not quite sure about this. Appropriate Adults may need to ensure they have these explained to them by the officers if they are not familiar with that police station.

What did create difficulties for them sometimes was being told things by the suspect which may cause moral difficulties for them in terms of confidentiality. They were both clear that they told suspects that they did not want to know whether they were guilty of an offence or not, as that was not their role. However, if a suspect did tell them something and someone else was at risk in some way, they were clear that they would have to pass this on and it would not create dilemmas for them.

Both thought that it is possible for Appropriate Adults to have preferences for, or prejudices against, certain types of suspects, and that this needs to be monitored by themselves in supervision, and counselling if necessary. When asked about the suspects they found most difficult to work with, they said that the most difficult ones are those who are obstructive and/or violent.

In relation to these stresses, David spoke of having been involved in one particularly difficult situation he attended where a young man who had been suspected of carrying out a murder had subsequently taken his own life. He said the thoughts and feelings which can arise from having been involved in such a situation could continue for a long time. MIND does have counsellors who they can approach if need be over their stresses.

Reasons for volunteering as an Appropriate Adult
When asked about reasons for volunteering, David said that initially it was after he had taken early retirement and started working in a MIND day centre. He had heard about the Appropriate Adult scheme and thought it was something he could contribute to. He had heard in the Day Centre service users were often arrested by the police at evenings and weekends, and kept in custody for long periods without the protection of an Appropriate Adult; this he though unfair and unjust. He recalled that initially he had felt very apprehensive in the first interview; the hustle and bustle of the police station, the smell of it, trying to gain entry, trying to carve out physical and psychological space, on his own and feeling unconfident about this; he found the whole experience very off-putting. Both Ron and David said it was important to have a proper and full induction and a chance to consult with members of staff of the scheme for their support. They believed it was important not to feel isolated and to know that people would have time to talk with you, in a suitable venue. Shadowing of experienced Appropriate Adults, and familiarisation with the police station was seen to be important.

David said that the reason he keeps on doing it is because if he gets a 'good result', as he put it, then he felt he had helped someone and went out 'walking on air'. He said the custody officers quite often make a point of saying 'thank you' afterwards and that it was also gratifying to know that he had helped the process along in a way that he thought opened up communication and under-standing between the different people involved. Both had encountered officers who seemed sensitive to the stresses on the Appropriate Adults.

An issue that was raised by the NCH Appropriate Adults was also mentioned by Ron and David. The fact that they are not paid and they are there by choice can often mean that suspects are better able to relate to volunteers without the other agendas that can inevitably arise with others, such as Social Services social workers who may carry out the role.

The normal length of attendance at interviews was only a few hours, but David had known of someone involved in a two day case, and he had been involved for over 4 days in one particular case. This was where a man with a mental health disorder had allegedly murdered a person and had then taken his own life whilst in custody. David's concern was where he could 'download', as he put it, the feelings about this. He said that 'gory ones go with you' and it is important to try to unwind. His way of doing this is to go out again as quickly as possible on a less serious case. David also made the point that the work can be very demanding, and it is important to recognise when you need time out from the work. He said that he had discovered this two years ago after undertaking over 100 interviews.

Key points made by volunteers from both schemes
From these structured discussions with the volunteers, a number of key themes became clear which have a bearing on their effectiveness in trying to fulfil the role as a volunteer within such a scheme. The themes raised centred on police attitudes and practices; suspects' views of them in their role, and the effect on outcomes; confidentiality; training and support; and commit-ment to their work.

These themes were:
- The importance of clarity of role and independence from police and social services and the voluntary nature of the role. Most of the Appropriate Adults believed that they gained greater trust from suspects, if not necessarily the police, because of these factors. This meant that the suspect knew that the volunteer was only focusing on them and their situation and needs at that time. Social workers, for example, may have other roles, demands and sets of relationships to think about as well

- The importance of the ability and willingness of the manager to support the Appropriate Adult individually. The manager needs to be able to pick up general themes and problems in the work in order to be able to represent these and facilitate change where needed with, for example, social services and police representatives on steering groups. The role can be quite isolated, but this seemed not to bother most volunteers; what is important is the security and confidence gained from the knowledge acquired during training and ongoing support

- Understanding how suspects may be experiencing the detention, and the stress this can put on them

- The extraordinary level of commitment of volunteers to justice being done for suspects in relation to their vulnerabilities and their welfare

- The importance of feeling confident in managing the relationship with police, and the need for a good relationship with them, but also knowing how to be assertive at times.

- Knowing how to challenge police behaviour when it is seemingly pressuring the suspect.

- Volunteers clearly saw their role as an advocate for the interests of the suspects.

- A very apparent pride in carrying out the role effectively for the suspect

- The vital importance of all involved showing respect and not disdain for each other- police to suspects and Appropriate Adults, Appropriate Adults towards police and suspects, even when assertiveness was needed.

References

Pearse, J and Gudjonsson, G (1996) 'How appropriate are appropriate adults?' *Journal of Forensic Psychiatry* 7(3) pp. 570–80.

Chapter 12
Appropriate Adult Schemes for Vulnerable Adults

Andrew Strong

The Southampton MIND Appropriate Adult Scheme

Dedicated schemes providing trained Appropriate Adults have emerged across the country over the past 5 years. Most have used volunteers for the majority of their referrals.

The Southampton MIND scheme was one of the first of its kind. It started in July 1994 following research conducted at Southampton in 1992 by an Approved Social Worker whose role was to develop a diversion scheme. The research cross-referenced 3,000 custody records (about 25 per cent of the annual total detained at the central custody centre) with the Social Services database of clients. It found that 8 per cent of custody records referred to persons who were clients of social services because of a mental disorder.

The social worker, who visited the station regularly in the course of the research, was being asked more and more frequently to act as an Appropriate Adult for vulnerable detained adults. This was compromising her role both as a diversion worker but particularly as an Approved Social Worker as she was also expected to assess people under the Mental Health Act 1983 for possible compulsory admission to a hospital.

Subsequently, Southampton MIND were approached and a multi-agency steering group was established to look at the possibility of setting up an Appropriate Adult scheme. This coincided with the availability of grants from the Mental Health Foundation who, on behalf of the Home Office, were looking to fund new and innovative mentally disordered offenders' schemes across the country. A successful bid to the Mental Health Foundation enabled Southampton MIND to set up a 2-year pilot scheme that was independently evaluated by the Criminology Department at Loughborough University.

After a successful pilot, the scheme's funding was taken over by Southampton City and Hampshire County Councils. It now operates in Southampton, south-west Hampshire and, as of late 1999, Basingstoke, covering five designated police stations.

The scheme's annual referral figures give some indication of its development and growing importance:

1994 = 37
1995 = 216
1996 = 355
1997 = 519
1998 = 655
1999 = 880

The projected figure for 2000 is over 1,000 referrals.

How the scheme operates

Two members of staff, a manager and project worker, co-ordinate the scheme which cannot operate with fewer than 10 volunteers. Staff are responsible for recruiting, training and managing volunteers, acting in the role when required and referring clients on to relevant agencies. In addition, the manager has a regular training and awareness-raising role.

All volunteers are offered one-to-one support or supervision. Bi-monthly support meetings are also held for volunteers to come together to talk through issues and listen to an invited speaker on relevant topics. A minimum of one session a week is expected of each volunteer. There are two sessions to cover each day, 0730–1700 hours and 1700–2300 hours. The scheme operates every day. The Hampshire Constabulary Force Control Room is issued with a rota from Southampton MIND and, at a custody officers' request, will page the person on duty. Calls do not have to go via a member of staff or through Social Services. The scheme operates autonomously but is accountable to the monitoring groups.

The monitoring group now meets twice a year in Southampton and quarterly in Basingstoke. Southampton MIND provide figures from their database on:

- number of referrals over a defined period
- number of referrals at each station
- days and times called
- average length of time spent at the police station
- age-range, ethnicity and gender of clients
- alleged offence categories
- vulnerability categories
- outcomes

Qualitative evaluation is also requested via occasional questionnaires to police officers and solicitors. Anecdotal evidence suggests that client feedback is generally positive.

Southampton MIND will refer clients on to relevant social care agencies, where necessary, if they provide written consent.

Finally, if necessary, the scheme will also attend for vulnerable victims or witnesses whilst they are making their statements to the police.

The matters discussed below are based on the experiences of the Southampton MIND scheme.

Important points for setting up a scheme

1. To establish a quality sustainable service it must be established from the outset, whatever the locality, that the local authority is interested in funding a possible scheme. Individuals should not proceed without this likelihood. The first step would be to 'sound out' the relevant Service Manager and then to establish a multi-agency group which includes the Police, Health, Social Services, Probation and the voluntary sector.

   Of course, as is often the case, the local authority might be the first to propose the idea, usually in response to pressures on their adult services to attend police stations. Local authorities do not have a statutory duty to provide Appropriate Adult services for vulnerable adults and being asked to do so can be difficult when resources are already stretched with priority work. According to an analysis of Southampton MIND's 3,000 referrals, an Appropriate Adult can expect to spend, on average, 3 hours at a custody centre.

2. Invite someone from an established scheme along to explain the advantages and methods of working.

3. Do some research on the prevalence of mentally disordered offenders in police custody, nationally and locally.

4. Gain the support in principle of police officers at the appropriate level within the constabulary.

5. Decide whether the service is to be managed by a voluntary sector organisation or by social services, and who will actually carry out the role (usually this will be volunteers).

6. Establish a budget which of course would depend on the proposed size of the service and who is managing it. Social Services will lead on this whilst other statutory organisations should also contribute.

7. Draw up a service specification and ensure the steering group agrees to its contents. Propose a 2-year pilot scheme. Use other schemes as models. Social Services should lead on this.

8. Invite tenders, if necessary or recruit staff within an identified organisation that will undertake the provision of the service.

9. When practitioners are in post, change the steering group into a monitoring group and review targets quarterly, as set out previously in this chapter. This group has a vital role during the pilot phase.

Advantages

Southampton MIND has found the following to be the key advantages of a designated scheme.

Response times

All persons detained in police custody, according to paragraph 1.1 of Code C, PACE 1984 Codes of Practice, 'must be dealt with expeditiously and released as soon the need for detention has ceased to apply'.

No party involved would wish for a vulnerable person to be held longer than is necessary. However, custody officers often have difficulty in identifying a relative or professional who is able or willing to attend without undue delay. It is not uncommon for the custody process to be delayed for several hours before someone can attend. Vulnerable adults often object to a relative attending whilst Social Services departments are often reluctant to send someone unless the detained person is well known to them.

The belief is, where Appropriate Adults are more easily obtainable, that officers are more likely to err on the side of safety and request one. This means that more vulnerable adults will have their rights and welfare protected as specified in the PACE Codes.

A dedicated scheme should be (and usually is) able to provide an Appropriate Adult when required. Southampton MIND can usually respond immediately if necessary.

Priorities:eligibility criteria

In the case of a vulnerable adult, a social worker may object to attending or staying to act as an Appropriate Adult for someone who does not meet their department's agreed eligibility criteria for referral even though PACE may require that someone attends.

A dedicated scheme should not have to use eligibility criteria unless resource constraints dictate otherwise. The scheme would then be more accessible, reducing the risk of a vulnerable person being detained in breach of the PACE Codes by not having an Appropriate Adult (*R. v. Kenny*, Court of Appeal 1993).

Southampton MIND operate within very broad 'vulnerability' referral criteria which encourages the police to call them if they have *any doubt* (Code C, 11.B) about a person's welfare. This means that the person does not necessarily have to suffer from a mental disorder: they could, for example, simply be unable to read or write. Unit Commander John Pearse's (1995) definition of psychological vulnerability is helpful here: any factor, or combination of factors, that could have a bearing on the reliability of a confession or incriminating statement. Granted, this is very much a police perspective concerned with safeguarding evidence, but because it avoids references to diagnoses or priorities it is helpful to police officers who receive little or no training on identification of mental disorder.

Adequate training
Southampton MIND takes the view that dedicated schemes send better trained Appropriate Adults than local authorities do. It is a false notion that volunteers are not professionals and are therefore less equipped to cope with the demands of the role. Volunteers also have the added advantage of being completely independent: they are there because they want to be.

Southampton MIND provides thorough training and has volunteers who have acted in the role on over 150 occasions. Applicants, who do not need to have had any previous experience, must complete application forms and be interviewed, have 2 referees and agree to a police check. If all is satisfactory, they will receive four 3-hour sessions of theory on mental health and learning disability, and two on the role itself. Alongside these sessions they will have at least two opportunities to shadow an experienced volunteer at a custody centre in order to put the theory into a practical context. When they are comfortable they will go out alone.

Practice guidelines for Appropriate Adults are as crucial as the training. Southampton MIND uses guidelines to emphasise boundaries and their position regarding confidentiality and disclosure (given that information which passes from a suspect to an Appropriate Adult may have to be disclosed under certain circumstances).

117

General

Dedicated schemes have Appropriate Adult work as their focus. This means they are able to commit to the demands upon their time which social services teams are stretched to cover. Proper training means that those acting in the role are aware of the potential difficulties. This and prompt response times should create a good working relationship with the police especially where an officer of at least the rank of Inspector is a member of a multi-agency group steering the work (a vital part of any successfully managed scheme).

Southampton MIND have seen their annual referral rate for vulnerable adults soar as result of both good practice in the custody centre and regular training or awareness sessions with police officers.

A dedicated scheme will also help to increase awareness of mental health amongst police officers and, alongside a dedicated local authority diversion scheme, will assist in promoting alternatives to prosecution where appropriate.

Contributors' Details

Keith Baldwin is a Superintendent in the Hertfordshire Constabulary, where he has worked since 1970, eventually holding the post of Divisional Commander. He has served in various departments, including Community and Race Relations.

Debra Fearns Hansen is Senior Lecturer in the Department of Health and Social Care at the University of Hertfordshire. She is a Registered Nurse (learning disabilities) and teaches learning disability nursing across pre and post registration courses. Debra recently completed her MA in Health and Social Policy, carrying out research into how custody officers recognise vulnerability, especially people with learning disabilities. She is continuing working on issues for people with learning disabilities in the Criminal Justice system.

Grethe Hansen is Senior Lecturer in Mental Health at the University of Hertfordshire. She specialises in inter-professional working and co-ordinates the inter-agency Hertfordshire Mental Health Joint Training and Work Force Development Unit. She has also carried out extensive consultancy and research projects on collaborative working in mental health with statutory and independent agencies in Hertfordshire and London.

Brian Littlechild has been a social worker, emergency duty worker and manager in a number of social services departments in London and East Anglia. He is currently Associate Head of Department of Health and Social Care at the University of Hertfordshire, where he is also a member of the Centre for Community Research. In addition to providing training and consultancy, he has published widely on the appropriate adult role, including the 1996 British Association of Social Workers book, *The Police and Criminal Evidence Act 1984: the role of the appropriate adult*.

John Pearse is a serving officer with the Metropolitan Police Service and he has worked in London for over a quarter of a century. He is currently Unit Commander, Special Intelligence Section (part of the Criminal Intelligence Branch of New Scotland Yard). His interest in the Appropriate Adult field was stimulated by his involvement with a live armed robbery case in the early 1980s, which raised issues concerning vulnerability, and led him to undertake a Ph.D. in Forensic Psychology, as well as numerous publications. Some publications include: Pearse, J (1995) 'Police Interviewing: The Identification of

Vulnerabilities' *The Journal of Community and Applied Social Psychology* (5) pp 147–59. Pearse, J and Gudjonsson, G H (1996) 'How Appropriate are Appropriate Adults?' *Journal of Forensic Psychiatry* 7(3) 570–80.

Andrew Strong has considerable experience of managing Appropriate Adult schemes with Southampton and New Forest MIND. He has been involved in developing the scheme as well as making presentations on their work at a number of regional and national conferences.

INDEX